CONTROL YOUR FUTURE

How to Profit From the Financial Services Revolution

Robert W. MacDonald, CLU

THE NATIONAL UNDERWRITER COMPANY
CINCINNATI, OHIO

DEDICATION

To the builders of the life insurance industry—The agents of yesterday, today and tomorrow.

TABLE OF CONTENTS

INTRODUCTION

When I was a very young man just starting out as an agent, one of the grizzled, older agents in my agency came to me one day and said, "Son, by the time you're my age, the insurance industry will have been taken over by the government, and you'll be working for some bureaucrat." That was 20 years ago. And, except for the fact that I have reached the age of my advisor, 42, I'm not working for the government any more than anyone else who pays taxes.

Today, the life insurance industry exists almost as it did in 1965, except that it's a whole lot bigger and more successful. Yet, there are still people forecasting the extinction of the agent. There are those who say the agent is an endangered species who will not survive the revolution in financial services.

Robert E. Evans, CLU, general agent for Berkshire Life, best expressed the fear and anxiety of many agents when he wrote, "Frankly, I'm scared. In more than 20 years since I entered the life insurance business, I've watched my profit margins shrink alarmingly. But unless I misread the signs, what we've seen in the past few years is nothing compared with the threats to our livelihoods that lie ahead. So, I'm scared. And if you're not, perhaps you don't understand the problems we're facing."[1]

Mr. Evans and I may not agree as to how challenges to the agency system should be met, but we do agree that now is a very critical time in the history of the agent and the agency system. I believe the people who say the agent is passe′ are just as wrong as the person who advised me. However, that does not mean the agent of today does not face challenges. There are serious challenges. But we should not throw up our hands and desert the agent. In fact, there are outstanding opportunities for the agent who is flexible in his or her thinking and who views the unknown as a challenge rather than a threat.

The purpose of this book is to offer agents ideas and suggest actions they can take in response to changes taking place in the financial services industry. In this book, the agent will learn how to prepare for the future. I'll outline what I believe are the best ways for the agent to deal with the companies, the competition, and the consumer. The hope is that with these ideas the agent will not only be able to survive but will, in fact, thrive.

This book is dedicated to and aimed directly at the most important person in the life insurance industry—the agent. You won't find any surefire, hyped-up sales stories or "keep pluggin'" exhortations. Those things are fine, but we don't have time for that now. Rather, this book offers some candid, direct, and tough thoughts about the life insurance industry, the companies, and some of the so-called agent leaders. I suspect many in the industry will attack, ignore, or reject the ideas expressed in this book. That's fine with me. What the life insurance industry badly needs, however, is a diversity of ideas. For too long it seems as though all discussions in the life insurance industry have been conducted in an echo chamber. Only with a diversity of viewpoints can agents and companies fully explore the options available as we face changing times and increased competition.

I believe very few people in positions of leadership, responsibility, or authority have been completely honest with the agent. The time has passed when agents can rely on others to determine and protect their future. If agents are going to survive the revolution in financial services, they must begin that process by starting to make their own decisions about the future. Possibly my experience and insight gained from ten years as an agent and general agent, followed by ten years in home office management, can be of some help to agents as they chart their future.

Today's environment requires more from an agent than simply prospecting, selling and servicing clients. My stated objective will be reached if, 20 years from now, agents who read this book can look back and say, "Those who said the agent was extinct sure were wrong."

April, 1986 Robert W. MacDonald, CLU

[1] Robert E. Evans, CLU, "Rebates and Banks: More Threatening Than We Thought?" *Life Association News,* March 1985, p. 33.

CONTROL YOUR FUTURE

1

THE RELUCTANT REVOLUTION

In his novel *Good as Gold,* Joseph Heller created a professor whose credo was, "Every change is for the worse."[1] From my perspective, that professor would feel very comfortable working in the home offices of many life insurance companies. Let's face it, some of us in the life insurance industry don't like change. We don't encourage it, and when it comes, we sometimes don't even recognize it. When we do recognize it, we tend not to do anything about it. It is as if we think the waves of change will wash against the shore and then spill harmlessly back into the sea. However, these are dangerous times for those who stand still because the waves of change are hazardous. If unheeded, they can leave us drowning in our own inertia.

The life insurance industry's attempt to cling to the past rather than respond to the changes taking place in the financial services industry has forced the industry to become deeply embroiled in a revolution—two revolutions really. The industry has been forced to implement basic structural changes in products and, at the same time, has been drawn into the restructuring of the entire financial services industry. As a result, there have been more changes in the life insurance industry during the last five years than had occurred in the previous 50. New product development, of course, was essential if we were to have a chance at regaining the consumer's confidence and savings dollar. As we all know, some dramatic product changes have already taken place.

The dominant products of our industry today were, only a few years ago, just a glint in the eyes of a few progressive actuaries (if there is such a thing as a progressive actuary.) For the first time in this century, traditional whole life is not the dominant product of our industry. There are those who said that without whole life, both the insurance industry and the American way of life would be ruined. And there are those who didn't even bother to make the distinction. Yet, some of those who predicted doom are today making money they wouldn't be making without these new products. And, many of you reading this book may actually be thriving because of the product revolution.

There are a few companies still trying to hold onto the products of the past, but then, there are still a few companies that repair wagon wheels and make buggy whips. These companies will try to hold on for a long time, but I predict that sooner or later they will recognize it's hard to sell Veg-o-Matics in a Cuisinart society. They will come around to the realities of the times for if they don't, they stand a good chance of becoming very, very quiet companies. Certainly, one result of the product revolution is very clear: never again will the life insurance industry seriously introduce a product that is not interest sensitive.

Of course, as with most revolutions, this one did not come without a little bloodshed. Many in the life insurance industry were very content selling traditional products in the traditional way. Industry leaders tried to survive by selling the same old products and asking the agents to operate the same old way, even as the rest of the financial services industry evolved around us.

Life insurance executives felt pretty content about a world filled with gullible consumers that would allow them to sell products with stone age benefits in a space age world. And they had an equally comforting image of the agent as an all-believing person who would sell whatever was handed to him. But the real world changed. Economic uncertainty, punctuated by soaring inflation and volatile interest rates, resulted in a better educated marketplace. Consumers became more aware of the time value of money. In this new financial environment, they came to view life insurance not only as a form of protection, but as an investment, too. Before plunking down their money, consumers began asking tougher questions and demanding better value. Gone were the days when our industry was in the enviable position of being able to sell the products we wanted to sell rather than the products consumers wanted to buy.

Just as the consumer could not be fooled by the inaction of the industry leaders, agents also began to take notice of a shifting financial market. Agents were out in the field everyday and recognized the consumer was demanding more sophisticated, more competitive products. They perceived the difficulty in trying to make a living with products the consumer rejected as "out-of-date." When the agents tried to speak up, no one listened! As usual, the most important people in our business—the ones who meet the consumer face-to-face—were ignored because they were "just agents."

Despite what was happening in the real world, most companies simply kept operating the way they always had. They viewed their traditional products as somehow unique and unassailable. They tried nearly everything to protect this position—litigation, legislation, and advertising blitzes. They spread the word that the new products being introduced were inferior, and the agents selling them were branded as unprincipled entrepreneurs. Those who spoke out for better products and services were depicted as "anti-agent," "snake oil salesmen" and perpetrators of a "scam" on the insurance industry.

In the name of the agent, the consumer and, most of all tradition, these curators of the past did everything they could to keep the new products out of sight, if not out of mind. They spent millions of policyholder dollars trying to have Universal Life either outlawed or declared a tax cripple. As Stuart Kingston prophetically said in early 1982, "It is sad to see large Eastern mutuals and their agents indirectly suggesting tax penalties on Universal Life, which could spread to and hurt all policy forms."[2]

Remember the expensive, rather arrogant ads run by Mass(achusetts) Mutual suggesting that universal life would be a good product to buy only if they were selling it? And, of course, Mass Mutual was not selling universal life. Then there were the panicky Northwestern Mutual ads suggesting that people who purchased universal life might just as well buy a ticket on a roller coaster. (And people criticized ITT Life for its ads!) *The Wall Street Journal* summed up the attitude of many traditional companies when it said, "But for old-line mutual life insurance giants, who can't or won't sell the new policies and whose profitability is tied to conventional high-cost whole life insurance, the boom in Universal Life is ominous."[3]

It didn't happen, but it would not have been too farfetched to imagine Garry Silverlake, president of Old Time Mutual, standing before a screaming crowd of sneaker-clad home office executives at the annual meeting of the American Council of Life Insurance and intoning, "Extremism in the defense of whole life is no vice. . . and moderation in fighting new ideas is no virtue."

The efforts to stop the new products were real and got what they deserved—failure!—for they were not taken in the name of the consumer or the agent. They were taken to try to protect an industry that had grown lazy and non-competitive. The only result of these actions to preserve the status quo was to allow the consumer, once effectively served by us, to pass us by. At the same time, it put agents in the position of appearing to be out of step with the consumer. Looking back, we now know the stickiest problem facing the life insurance industry was not the obsolescence of the products. The biggest problem was that many of the leaders of our industry refused to accept the reality of changing consumer needs and desires. William J. Clark, president of Mass Mutual, was quoted at the American Society of CLU (ASCLU) 1981 convention when he noted that whole life's only current problems were, "an antiquated federal tax law and policy loan interest rates which make no sense in a high interest environment."[4] Indeed, with such attitudes, the industry and its agents took on an appearance of being anti-consumer.

If you doubt this, review these results from a 1983 *Monitoring the Attitudes of the Public"* (MAP) survey conducted by the American Council of Life Insurance. Less than four out of ten insurance consumers believe that life insurance companies give them their money's worth; only three of every ten agree that life insurance companies have high ethical codes; less than three of ten think life insurance companies have been doing a good job of educating the public about life insurance; only 15 percent think life insurance offers their money protection; when rating financial vehicles that help protect against inflation, consumers placed life insurance well behind savings accounts, individual retirement accounts, all-savers certificates, money market funds and stocks.[5]

The actions, or rightly the non-actions, of the life insurance industry created a perception on the part of the consumer that a better return on the savings dollar was available elsewhere than from the life insurance companies. Consumers, in effect, told us to offer something better or they would find someone who would. Many industry leaders recognized the signals, but few did anything about the problem. For the most part, all we saw was defensive posturing and holier-than-thou pious platitudes.

Traitor . . . Traitor . . . Traitor

The experiences I had with the traditionalists of the life insurance industry were similar to what others encountered. In January of 1982, ITT Life made an announcement that rocked the life insurance industry. ITT Life declared that because the consumer was increasingly rejecting traditional whole life insurance, we had decided to stop selling the product. We believed that unless there were a rapid and radical change in product, our company, our agents and our industry would continue to lose the confidence of the consumer. As we pointed out then, neither the companies nor the agents were to blame for a good product going bad. The culprits were volatile interest rates, surging inflation, and intense competition from other sectors of the financial services industry.

Purely from a marketing standpoint, ITT Life was vindicated when 1982 sales results for the life insurance industry were, in the words of *The Wall Street Journal,* ". . . the worst in recent memory." As the article explained, "After a decade in which premium income from sales of new individual life policies grew 6% to 9% annually, premium income was nearly flat last year (1982) at $5.68 billion, up only 0.5% . . . The news was even gloomier for sales of individual whole life policies, long the bread and butter of the life insurance industry. Premiums from new sales of traditional whole life policies dropped 12% in 1982 from a year earlier. And whole life's share of new individual life sales fell to 55% from 63%."[6]

But the leaders of the industry and those they control responded to our actions with self-righteous indignation. How could we even dare to question the great American institution of life insurance? From the reaction we received, you might have assumed we had come out and said, "God is dead." For some, saying whole life was dead amounted to nearly the same thing. Ads were taken out denouncing our position; articles were written talking about our desperate, misguided action.

You should have seen some of the letters I received. One guy wrote, "We will be looking for you." I was called the "Antichrist" of the life insurance industry. One person wrote and said we were the "cesspools of the life insurance industry." There was even a letter to the American Society of CLU suggesting my designation be revoked. One of the letters I enjoyed most came from a company president who said, "You are wrong about whole life, and to prove it, I have just bought another policy."

Of course, this wasn't the first time those who stepped out of line were attacked by industry traditionalists. You may recall that in the early 1960s, a few agents attempted to become licensed by the National Association of Securities Dealers (NASD) so they could sell mutual funds. Do you remember the industry reaction? Many agents who became NASD licensed were terminated! I've even been told of an individual who was denied the presidency of the National Association of Life Underwriters (NALU) only because he happened to be licensed to sell both life insurance and mutual funds. How times have changed. Today there are companies that virtually require agents to become NASD licensed.

The life insurance industry responded to our message in its normal, negative way but we received another type of reaction as well. It was a reaction that many of our critics feared because it came from the very people to whom we were aiming our message—the consumers and the agents. I received letters from agents all over the country thanking me for speaking out and saying the things those in the field knew to be true. They told me of the difficult times trying to make a living selling the same, old products and the frustration over the feeling that no one seemed to be listening to them.

Most of those issues are behind us. Today, the product revolution is, for the most part, over. We now have a good idea as to the types of products that will be sold in the future. Many companies that fought hard against the new products have now added them to their portfolio.

A number of companies that, just a few years ago, were claiming there was nothing wrong with traditional whole life have instituted patch-up jobs on their existing policies. This action would be like selling black and white television sets in the 1950s. When color became a reality, they claimed it was a passing fad or dangerous to one's health. When this approach didn't work, they offered red and green plastic to put in front of the picture tube and called them color TVs. You could hardly blame someone who had never seen color TV for thinking the plastic had upgraded the set. But the consumer won't be fooled for long. As the years pass, whole life, upgraded or not, will be about as common as black and white TVs.

How many companies that four years ago tried to legislate universal life out of existence are today claiming they invented it?

There will be many product refinements in the future, but the major changes have been made. It's like going from the horse and carriage to the automobile. The first models of the auto were not nearly as good as they are today, but the concept was in place. Once the corner was turned, there was no going back. From a product standpoint, the life insurance industry has turned the product corner. Traditional whole life will have its deserved place in the Life Insurance Hall of Fame which, by the way, would best be placed on Asylum Street in Hartford.

But We've Always Done It That Way

Does that mean no more or, at least, gradual change in the future? From a product standpoint, that may be true. From here on, unless they buy term policies, consumers will share, almost fully, in our investment risks. Policyholders will win when we win, and lose when we lose. For better or worse, we live amidst floating interest rates and it's now recognized that we have to design our products with this fundamental reality in mind.

In the future, consumers will be able to decide for themselves the degree of risk they like. Soon we will allow the consumers to direct the cash value portion of their policies into investment funds that meet their objectives. Policyholders may opt for the safety of government-backed treasury bills, or for more speculative and potentially larger returns in stocks, bonds, gold, diamonds, commodities and real estate. Future policies will evolve toward variable premiums and variable benefits. For example, the industry will issue a policy that fixes a certain death benefit as a floor, with all additional benefits above that floor tied to market performance of invested premiums.

Consumers now understand floating rate certificates of deposit and floating rate money market funds. It's only a matter of time before they also become comfortable with floating premiums and benefits. This new understanding gives the insurance industry a chance to turn a long-standing liability into an asset. We have always had a well-deserved reputation for effectively managing our investments, but there has been some feeling that our investment success came at the expense of the consumer.

Now we have the chance to turn this around, to share our skills with the public. The time is coming when a great many of us will match the brokers and the mutual funds in offering a wide array of protection and investment vehicles. However, because the major structural changes have already been made, future changes will be much more evolutionary. It will be a different story for other changes in the life insurance industry. The real revolution is just getting started. As that famous sage once said, "Hold on to your hats. . . you ain't seen nothin' yet!"

An industry that was once characterized by its staid, stable and, let's admit it, boring ways, is no longer. Aggressiveness in the life insurance industry can no longer be defined as offering real leather rather than vinyl policy jackets. The operative word is change—dramatic, rapid, convulsive, real and continuing change. The speed, pace and impact of the changes we are seeing will not go away. If anything, the cycle of change will accelerate. Many in our industry view this activity with fear and trepidation. For them, any change and any messenger of change is viewed as a threat. In their eyes the future appears almost as though it's a dare, a line drawn in the dirt that only a desperate person will cross.

A good example of this attitude was demonstrated by Edward Keenan, editor of *Life Association News,* when he wrote, "Insurance companies must beware of change, because they manufacture products which come in and go out of style. Product peddlers must beware of change because they live by the very elements which come and go. But agents who sell knowledge of the financial scene and willingness to help people solve their problems, need not, and, in fact, cannot change."[7]

For many in our industry, the past is a Linus blanket to security. Never wanting to reach out toward what appears to be a different, if not totally unknown future, they react by clinging tightly to the past. They strike out at anything having to do with this unwanted interloper called change. This approach may make us feel secure now, but the problem is, if we only think about yesterday, we stand a strong chance of losing tomorrow. Tradition is necessary; I'm all for it. Let's remember, however, that tradition is something to build upon, not rest on. There is too much at stake for us to allow tradition to become an excuse for complacency.

Many in our industry act as though the only thing we have to fear is change itself. That's just not right. The biggest threat posed by change is the failure to recognize it. We must understand that change is not the enemy. The enemy is blind resistance to change. Change is neutral. It's neither good nor bad. How we react to change is what determines its impact on our lives.

I'm suggesting that we don't have to be intimidated by change. Those of us in the life insurance industry are presented with the opportunity to determine how change will impact our destiny. Agents can take steps to make sure they continue to have the opportunity to use their talent, the opportunity to enhance their success, the chance to ride the waves of change, and not be wiped out by them. We have the power to harness change and ride it to a positive future. The alternative is to be trampled by it. Each and every one of us has the power to shock the future rather than have the future shock us. We can use this power to initiate rather than react to change. To start, we must view change not as a threat but as an opportunity to step boldly into the future. William Jennings Bryan, the 19th century Populist leader, never sold a life insurance policy, but he did leave a message for those facing today's challenges. He said, "Destiny is not a matter of chance, it is a matter of choice. It is not a thing to be waited for, it is a thing to be achieved."

Chapter I Notes

[1] Joseph Heller, *Good as Gold,* (Simon and Schuster, New York) 1979.

[2] Stuart Kingston, "More on Universal Life," *National Underwriter,* Life and Health edition, January 16, 1982, p. 11.

[3] Daniel Hertzberg, "Insurers Split Over Benefits of Offering Universal Life," *The Wall Street Journal,* September 3, 1981, p. 11

[4] David C. Jones, "Clark: Whole Life Flexible, Durable," *National Underwriter,* Life and Health edition, November 21, 1981, p. 1.

[5] "Monitoring the Attitudes of the Public," American Council of Life Insurance, 1983.

[6] Daniel Hertzberg, "Life Insurers' Sales of Individual Policies in 1982 Were the Worst in Recent Memory," *The Wall Street Journal,* May 4, 1983.

[7] Edward Keenan, "Unchanging Times," *Life Association News,* April 1984, p. 4.

2

IF YOU MAKE A MISTAKE—BLAME SOMEONE

There is no doubt the product revolution was traumatic. Many had the feeling their whole life was being undermined by termites or invaded by some strange universal power. Moving from a comfortable, traditional product to an entirely new concept would be difficult even under the best of conditions. The life insurance industry, though, had to make the change in almost the blink of an eye.

In 1980, less than two percent of all sales were modern interest sensitive products. By 1985, many predicted the new products would capture over 50 percent of the market. That is tremendous growth in an industry as large as life insurance. Despite the upheaval, basic product changes are behind us, and we have survived. Now with barely time to catch our breath, the second phase of the life insurance revolution is upon us. If you thought the product revolution was fun, you'll love what's going to happen next. This new phase will affect agents even more than the change in products. The outcome of this revolution will go to the very core of the insurance industry and will determine whether agents will survive.

The biggest, single issue facing the life insurance industry today is not what products we are going to be selling, but how they will be sold. The agency system of distribution has served the life insurance industry and the consumer for over 125 years. During that period, there have been many challenges to the system, but none more serious than the one it's facing today. Simply put, today's competitive realities are challenging the life insurance industry to improve the way products are distributed to the consumer.

One can see that the classic career agency system is in trouble simply by counting the number of companies still using it. Some experts agree that real agent income has, for the last ten years, barely kept pace with inflation. Prior to the introduction of universal life, there were indications that real agent income was actually declining. Fewer companies are recruiting new people to sell life insurance. If the individuals recruited and licensed by the A.L. Williams organization were eliminated (which is what many would like to do), the last few years would show a reduction in the number of active agents. It has been reported that 10 companies out of more than 1,800 account for more than half the total number of people recruited into life insurance sales. The number of policyholders allowing their policies to lapse has increased dramatically in the last few years. As a result, it's much more difficult for agents to count on steady, long-term income.

These, however, are only symptoms of a problem. The real problem with the agency system can be summed up in one word—productivity. It costs a large amount of money to get an agent in front of a prospective customer. Working under the present system, the typical agent is not able to see enough people, or sell enough volume to assure survival in a very competitive financial services world. Even as defenders of the agency system, we must recognize that the system is costly and not very efficient. In fact, one would be hard pressed to come up with a more costly way of distributing products to the consumer. Any product that has over 1,800 manufacturers and 250,000 distributors either is in very high demand or is being distributed inefficiently. We all know the demand level for life insurance.

The agency system is inefficient, not because of the agent, but because the agent is asked to perform all phases of the sale. The agent must search out people to talk with, convince the prospect to buy the product and then service the policyholder after the sale. Two reasons for the inefficiency are that even though agents are very good at selling, most tend not to be very good at prospecting, and they don't like servicing. (Two good reasons why I'm in the home office.)

The inherent weaknesses in the agency system have always been with us, but it was not until recently that they were recognized as problems. A high cost distribution system can be effectively masked if: 1) the product being sold is unique; 2) there is little, if any, real competition; 3) the products sold have very high margins; 4) use for the product continues to grow and; 5) the salespeople are imbued with a missionary zeal to sell the product.

For more than a century, the life insurance industry has been fortunate to have most of these conditions working for it. The product being sold was unique. While the industry developed and grew, there were no other financial products offered that would protect against premature death and, at the same time, provide for the accumulation of capital. For most of the last century, premature death was a real concern. In the middle of the 19th century, only 45 people out of 100 would live to age 55. Infant and maternal death rates were as high as 35 percent. In 1985 those numbers look frighteningly ludicrous. Today, the chances of a baby surviving to age 55 are nearly 90 percent. The chances of survival to age 65 are more than 75 percent.

As was pointed out at the Life Office Management Association (LOMA) Human Resources Forum in April of 1985, death was an ever-present reality—to every social class, and at every stage of life—during the 18th and 19th centuries. "It was that death-obsessed society in which the North American Life Insurance industry took root and experienced its first explosive period of growth."[1]

As the life insurance industry developed, there were very few financial alternatives available to compete for the consumers' savings or investment dollar. Quoting again from the LOMA conference, ". . . the people of the last century (who) were obsessed by their own mortality, and demonstrated that obsession in their elaborate mourning dress and rituals. Life insurance was presented as a sacred duty, and people began to prepare for death in financial as well as religious terms."[2]

This lack of competition, combined with a strong feeling for the product among the consumers, meant the policies could be, and were so structured, that the consumer bore nearly all sales and administrative costs in the early years. Probably, any favorable margins that emerged in the later years went to the company rather than the consumer. Many religions would thank God for missionaries with the zeal of life insurance agents.

As the American population and economy grew, so did life insurance and its perceived need. A very favorable set of market factors allowed the life insurance industry to grow and prosper despite a distribution system that chewed up people faster than the Russian front; a distribution system that considered one sale per week not only above the norm, but almost a goal.

Those conditions exist no longer. The free ride has ended. It was the introduction of interest sensitive products that exposed the high cost of the traditional agency distribution system. The rocks were always in the harbor, but whole life was a high tide that allowed the industry to float above and ignore the danger. While many fought introduction of the new products simply because they did not want change, there were others who recognized that because of lower profit margins, the interest sensitive products could not support the traditional agency distribution system. Lynn Brenner made the point in the *Institutional Investor* when she wrote, "Given the profitability of whole life, it's not really surprising that so many industry leaders have clung to it. . . despite the clear and mounting evidence that consumers are disenchanted. In fact, it virtually supports the agency systems on which these companies depend. . ."[3]

Whole life was designed with the agency system in mind. The product design had built-in margins that allowed the companies to compensate for agency system inefficiencies. Whole life was also structured in a way that allowed old policies to help pay the cost of selling the new policies. Since whole life costs and benefits were based on guarantees, the premiums could be conservatively high and the benefits conservatively low. Due to the lack of any real competition for the life insurance industry, any improvement over the conservative assumptions could be held for the benefit of the company. Any improvement in mortality, reductions in costs, or increases in interest rates would help the company but not necessarily the consumer. As we know, all of these things happened.

Although delicately balanced, the agency system worked well for many decades. Suddenly, along came spiraling inflation and volatile interest rates. Right along with these conditions came deep recessions, a decline in real income, and recognition among consumers that one must get full value for what had truly become a hard-earned dollar. These experiences caused consumers to be much more discriminating with their money. This set the stage for a whole new generation of financial products that were designed to meet the financial problems of the late 20th century. Whole life, designed to meet the financial problems of the early 20th century, could not compete and, almost overnight, became obsolete.

Whole life was designed to compete against other whole life policies, but now the industry had to meet competition from a different type of product. With many new investment vehicles becoming available, people started to measure whole life not only as a form of protection, but as an investment as well. Just as the horse and carriage could not compete with the automobile, whole life could not compete effectively with the new financial products.

This point was underscored at the LOMA conference when it was said, "Where life insurance once occupied a unique—even a sacred—place in financial plans, it may now be viewed more as a useful financial instrument—one among many. It remains a necessity to guard against the potentially catastrophic financial loss resulting from premature death, but that risk is becoming peripheral to the *primary* financial objective, which is the accumulation of resources through saving and investment over a lengthy period of years.

"Even more disturbing, American data suggest that there has been a steady decline in the number of people who think of life insurance even as the preferred vehicle for protection against premature death—from 87% in 1968 to 76% in 1983. An astonishing 22% of Americans now believe that a *savings account* is the best way to provide that protection!"[4]

Despite these changing consumer objectives and perceptions, whole life remained the same as ever. It was a competitive product as long as you kept the consumer comparing it only to other whole life products. In an era when people had one job, one family, one prime rate, and one percent inflation, whole life fit well. But when people started looking at their life insurance and compared it to certificates of deposit, money market funds, mutual funds, and cash management accounts, they decided whole life did not measure up very well.

Unfortunately, we brought much of this problem upon ourselves because for years we sold life insurance as a "savings plan" and suggested it was a much better plan than those available from other sources. As long as the economy was stable or growing, the product maintained tax advantages and the competition was regulated as to the products it could offer. We had a strong story to tell and could win those battles.

While our leaders slept, though, this situation changed and suddenly we began losing the battles. Universal life and other interest sensitive products were designed to meet the consumer's new philosophy and the new competition, but not the needs of the distribution system. Now the industry was faced with a serious new problem. As Frank Tarbox, president of Penn Mutual said, "It has become clear to all of us that the mix of products and distribution methods designed for an era of economic stability are not well suited to a world of high inflation and interest rates."[5]

While many defended their resistance to the new products by claiming that universal life and its derivations were just an extension, or slight improvement on whole life, the fact of the matter is that a very basic concept had been turned upside down. Whole life was a product designed to provide financial protection against premature death that also happened to offer some investment return. The new products are designed to offer a good investment return that also happens to provide protection against premature death.

Since the emphasis of the new interest sensitive products is on investment return, any improvements on the assumptions in the policy, especially changes in interest rates, must be passed on to the consumer. Thus, events that increased the margins on whole life and made it so profitable act to decrease the margins on interest sensitive products. The basic problem is that we have introduced low-margin products designed to compete effectively against investment products, but we still use a distribution system that can only be supported by the old, high-margin whole life type products. Profit margins that were previously available to support the agency system are just not there with interest sensitive products. The very early universal life policies recognized this problem and took the simple solution of offering commissions more in line with the type of product it was—an investment. And you know the result. As much as agents recognized the need for better products, early interest sensitive offerings simply would not support the agency system and agents did not (could not) sell the products.

Why was E.F. Hutton Life the first to successfully market universal life? Does it have anything to do with access to large numbers of stockbrokers? It's interesting to note that E.F. Hutton's early sales were made by stockbrokers, not life insurance agents. Hartford Life was one of the first national companies to introduce universal life. They offered a competitive product, one that could match any money market fund, but the product did not sell. Why?

It paid commissions just like a money market fund! Universal life was a product whose time had come, but it did not take hold until companies selling it offered the policy with typical whole life commissions.

The Threat From Today's Universal Life

The idea of offering interest sensitive products was not only a good move, it was a necessity if the industry was to maintain any credibility with the consumer. However, the idea of selling the new products using the old distribution and compensation system is very dangerous. Sales are up and all looks very rosy today, but this is a Band-Aid approach and cannot continue for long. The situation we are in is a little like responding to a gas shortage by buying a high-powered, gas guzzler so we can get to the gas station faster.

I believe one of the biggest dangers facing the life insurance industry today may be universal life. The nature of the product combined with today's highly competitive market could result in the bankruptcy of many companies. The life insurance industry is presented with an interesting dilemma: if we keep selling interest sensitive products using the current agency distribution system and paying whole life commissions, there is a strong chance many companies will find themselves bankrupt. If commissions appropriate for the new products are paid, the agent cannot afford to sell them, and the companies will end up out of business.

This situation developed because the leaders of the life insurance industry never had to face real competition, and when it did arrive, they had no long-term strategy developed. Unless we get our act together and implement a real strategy, distribution costs will continue to soar, our products will become less competitive and agent income will continue to decline. The distribution issue is a critical one. I do not want to see the industry stick its head in the sand the way it did in response to the product deficiencies because the future of some 250,000 professionals is at stake.

On the whole, the industry is not making a very positive effort to address the distribution issue. One segment of the industry refuses to acknowledge the problem and goes along—business as usual—deluding itself and its agents. Another group recognizes the problem but throws up its hands and attempts to find ways to desert the agent. The leaders of the life insurance industry were caught off guard when the need for new products arose and, in response, are offering products that will not support both their need for profits and the distribution system. When the companies are forced to choose between their needs and the needs of their agents, I'm sure you know which side they will abandon. As a result, the agency system is under heavy attack. We hear the agent is an endangered species who will not survive the financial services revolution. We are told the agent is inefficient, not productive enough, and too costly. In short, the agent is outmoded.

Who do you think is making all the attacks on the agent? Is it the marketing specialists of the Harvard Business School? The stockbrokerage firms? Surely the banks are saying the agent is as outmoded as the teller! Perhaps the direct mail or telemarketing houses are saying the end of the agent is near. Or are the attacks coming from the consumer?

Those are all logical guesses, but they're wrong. In the famous words of Pogo: "We have met the enemy and they are us." Believe it or not, the heaviest attacks against the agent are not coming from the front, but from the back.

Those talking most about the demise of the agency system are the very same industry leaders who sat on their assets in their ivory towers during the product revolution. And today, they are trying to blame the agent for their failure to develop strategies that will allow the life insurance industry to compete effectively in the new financial services world. I've heard far too many industry executives—particularly those high salary guys who have never sold a policy—blame the agent for the distribution problem.

You don't believe me? You think I'm making this up? Try this on for size.

How many times in a sales interview have you used the phrase, "Mr./Ms. Prospect, if something should happen to you . . . ?" A hundred times? A thousand times? How many sales interviews have you conducted? Of course, what we're really saying is, "Mr./Ms. Prospect, if you should die . . ." Yet we don't say die because we've been conditioned to the fact that prospects don't like to talk about death, especially their own. So we use a euphemism that allows us to talk about death without actually saying the word.

Now, have you ever heard an insurance home office executive say, "We are very committed to our agents, but we are also looking at alternative or supplemental distribution systems"? Do you know what is really being said? The translation is, "We're trying to find a way to sell insurance without using our agents." The home office executive knows he can't talk about getting rid of agents, so he uses a euphemism for agent death—the alternative distribution system.

The June, 1985 issue of *Best's Review* surveyed 14 life insurance company executives. One of the questions asked was, "Has the life insurance industry reached the point where companies must seriously consider supplementary distribution channels in order to cut down on expenses?" Here are excerpts from the responses.

> John Creedon, president of Metropolitan Life: Yes, companies must consider supplementary distribution channels not only to cut expenses, but also to increase existing market share, penetrate new markets, and acquire the flexibility to compete in today's financial service business. The key is *supplementary* channels, rather than *alternative* channels, because you certainly cannot abandon what's been working well for you. Expenses are not necessarily the driving consideration since supplementary distribution channels are frequently not as efficient as well-managed traditional sys-

tems. At Metropolitan, we remain totally committed to our career agency system.[6]

> John Tait, president of Penn Mutual Life: The career agency system continues to be our primary distribution method because of the value it adds to Penn Mutual products. It allows us to meet our commitment to provide quality service for our clients. Our dilemma is that today, consumers do not always want to pay for this added value service. Many times they simply want a 'no-frills' competitive product and are willing to forego the time and expertise of our agents to get it. In these cases, it becomes essential for us to pursue sales opportunities through supplemental distribution systems, both to continue to support our agency while fulfilling clients' needs.[7]

George Orwell was not in the insurance business, but he certainly would be proud of logic that suggests the best way to support the agent is by using systems that eliminate the agent.

> L.J. Rowell, Jr., president of Provident Mutual Life: The industry reached the point of needing supplementary distribution channels some time ago. For companies having a career system as their primary source of distribution, it is absolutely imperative to develop additional distribution sources that will result in greater premium revenues at a lower unit cost, but hopefully will not reduce the career distribution system's effectiveness.[8]

> John T. Longmoore, president of John Hancock Variable Life: One must examine the existing distribution system closely to determine what it does well at a reasonable cost and try to minimize any inefficiencies. In addition, one must look at alternative approaches to distribution—direct mail solicitation and distribution through other retail systems such as securities brokers.[9]

> David D. Horn, senior vice president of Sun Life of Canada: Yes, and most aggressive companies have already done so.[10]

The executives quoted are good people, they represent fine companies, and I'm not attempting to pick on or embarrass them. There are many other quotes and companies I could point to as having the same, or even worse, attitudes toward the agent. The only question I raise is, if some industry leaders will make such statements in public, what are others saying and doing privately? *The Wall Street Journal* best summed up the attitude of many insurance executives and companies when it reported, "Increasingly, insurance companies have been offering a broader range of financial services and are trying to mass market products using direct mail, telephone solicitation and bigger advertising budgets. Their goal is to cut costs by bypassing the relatively expensive insurance agent distribution system."[11]

During some 20 years in the life insurance business, I've seen home office attitudes toward the agent go from feeling the agent is a "necessary evil" to simply "an evil." The company executives all say the nice sugarcoated things in public, but those are mostly empty words. You'd be surprised how many senior executives will admit privately that they'd love to do away with the agent. To me, the irony is that I've seen this private attitude expressed most often by executives of the leading career agent companies. In fact, not long ago I had representatives of one of the industry's oldest and largest career agent companies approach me to make a "special proposal." The gist of the offer was that this company would provide investment and administrative support for ITT Life's new products if I would agree to reinsure 30 percent of the business with their company. When I asked why they were making this offer, one of the executives bluntly said, "Our chairman believes this is a cheaper way to get business than through our agents." In essence, they wanted to write business but did not want to deal with the agent.

What's ironic is that when I'm giving speeches to agent groups, representatives of this company are some of my most vocal critics. What's more, there is a general agent for this company who belongs to the same country club as I, and he won't even talk to me.

Unfortunately, this attitude toward the agent is nothing new. The agent has always been the great whipping boy of the life insurance industry. Failures of the home office executives have always been blamed on the agent. It's a tradition in our industry to blame the agent for everything! If sales are down—blame the agent for not selling enough. If claims are up—blame the agent for doing a poor job of field underwriting. If expenses are a problem—blame the agent and cut commissions. If lapses are up—blame the agent for not doing a good job servicing.

For the First Time . . . Real Competition

Today the story is no different. The life insurance industry is experiencing something very unusual—competition. The industry leaders don't like the heat it generates, so they are responding by blaming the agent. They've grown lazy in an industry that has had no real competition. Now, I know you may be thinking, "That's not true. There has always been competition in the insurance industry." Not exactly. Agents have always competed against one another, but companies have competed with, not against, one another. This is a subtle but important distinction that must be understood.

The companies have worked together to keep competition out of their arena. The companies worked together to keep banks and other financial institutions out of insurance. The companies worked together to prevent unisex rates. The companies worked together to raise maximum policy loan interest rates. The companies worked together as a lobby trying to make sure state regulations fit their desires.

This attitude was best expressed in a letter written to me on January 31, 1984 by Richard S. Schweiker, president of the American Council of Life Insurance. (I later found out he wrote to all company presidents.) In the letter he said, "Never before in the history of the life insurance industry have we faced a greater challenge to our traditional ways of doing business than that which confronts us in 1984. The issues of taxation, risk classification (unisex) and bank deregulation, in particular, are of major concern to us and can most effectively be confronted by the business if we work together, if we act as one body and speak with one voice."

Agents can fight all they want with one another, but the companies really don't compete. They all use the same actuarial tables and interest assumptions. All product work is public record and companies gladly share marketing and product details. Agents worry about a penny here and a penny there in the dividend scale or premium rate, but as long as every company is selling basically the same product, each company knows it will get its share of the market.

If you're still not convinced, think back to some of your early training as an agent. Remember how you were told the prospect really didn't buy the product; instead, the prospect bought you and your service. What we were really being told was that the products being offered were indistinguishable. If we couldn't sell product competitiveness, then we had to do it with personality. (Maybe that's why I had such a short career as an agent!)

In the "good old days" of life insurance the saying was, "Companies differed only to the degree of enthusiasm exhibited by their sales force." Nevertheless, today there is real competition, and rather than responding in a way one might think logical, many industry leaders are lashing out the way they always have when things have gotten a little hot. They're saying the agent is the problem. Home office executives were asleep at the switch when the revolution in financial services roared by, but the agents are the ones who get tied to the tracks.

Many home office executives seem to be suffering from a form of distribution dyslexia. They see all the elements of the distribution problem but read everything backwards and upside down. The problem is not the agent. The problem is a lazy, myopic insurance industry that pays hypocritical lip service to agent loyalty while fighting changes to improve the system. The problem is an industry that seeks to mollify the agent while it plots systems that will allow them to eliminate the agent.

It seems some need to be reminded that it was the agent who built this industry. This industry was not built by the actuaries' lapse tables, or the underwriters' APS, or the investment people's interest charts; it certainly was not built in the company presidents' limousines. This industry was built on the hard work, dedication, perseverance and talent of millions of agents.

And let me tell you something! These so-called industry leaders are in for a big surprise. As hard as they try—and they are trying—they will not be able to survive without the agent. Life insurance is a very personal purchase—always has been and always will be. I don't believe people will ever be comfortable or well-served buying insurance from a machine, mannequin, or mail box. No matter how sweeping the changes in the life insurance industry may be, as long as people continue to breathe, bleed, and breed, the need for protection products isn't going to go away. And the need for people to sell these products isn't going to go away. Only the structure and method of sale will be different.

The changes taking place in the life insurance industry create some outstanding opportunities for competent, professional agents. The opportunities available today are probably better than they have ever been. Yet to take advantage of these opportunities, the successful agents are going to have to change their ways of thinking and operating. The old ways simply will not work in today's truly competitive world.

Those in positions of leadership in the life insurance industry have an obligation to the agents to find and develop systems that will allow them to apply their talents in a convenient, logical and efficient manner. Even if they don't want to do it for the agents, they better do it for themselves for they will not be able to survive without the agents.

To start, the industry must recognize that the distribution system, like the product until recently, is rooted in an era that has passed. It must be recognized that the problem is not the agent but the system under which the agent is asked to function. It has been estimated that the average successful agent spends about 80 percent of the time prospecting and servicing, and only 20 percent of the time selling. That's the real problem with the distribution system, and the industry should be working on ways to turn those numbers around.

Home office executives want to increase productivity and cut costs. That's fine, but I think the best way to do that is by helping the agents sell insurance more effectively, not reduce their income or try to find ways to get around or eliminate the agent. One of the industry's top priorities should be to find a way to help bring the customer to the agent, rather than take the agent to the customer. In this effort, we need to work with, not against the agents. The leaders of the insurance industry should stop blaming the agents for their own mistakes and start working with the agents to analyze how customers prefer to buy insurance and then adapt the systems accordingly. For agents to survive—and they must survive if the industry is to survive—we must find a way to help agents spend more time doing what they and only they can do. . .and that's sell life insurance.

Chapter II Notes

[1] John Panabaker, "Life Beyond the Great Divide," *1985 Life Office Management Association Human Resources Forum,* Denver, Colorado, April 22, 1985.

[2] *Ibid.*

[3] Lynn Brenner, "Can the Life Insurance Industry Survive?" *Institutional Investor,* September 1981, pp. 173-174.

[4] Panabaker, *op. cit.*

[5] Lois J. Lyons, "New Products: Who, What, When, Where and Which," *National Underwriter,* Life and Health edition, November 28, 1981, p. 4.

[6] "Life/Health Executives Speak Out," *Best's Review,* June 1985, pp. 36-37.

[7] *Ibid.,* p. 36.

[8] *Ibid.,* p. 37.

[9] *Ibid.,* p. 37.

[10] *Ibid.,* p. 36.

[11] "Travelers Corp. Hires Heilshorn to Direct Mass Marketing Unit," *The Wall Street Journal,* February 20, 1985.

3

WHO CARES ABOUT THE AGENT?

In 1982, Bobby D. Anderson, CLU, raised a very poignant question: "Government bureaucracies will look out for the clients, and most insurance companies will look out for themselves, but who cares about the agent?"[1]

Neither insurance companies, consumers or government agencies are the most important players in the struggle for agent survival. Nor are the presidents of insurance companies the key figures. No executive, no regulation, no consumer movement will determine whether agents survive. There is but one key player in the drama of agent survival—the agent!

If agents don't take swift and decisive action to protect their future, no one else will. There is no blue ribbon presidential task force or liberal think tank currently agonizing over the agent's well-being. There is, instead, a kind of social Darwinism at work here, a survival of the fittest and smartest agents. Those who survive the distribution revolution will be like those who survived the product revolution. The survivors will be those with the ability to change, the ability to try new things; those who find stimulation instead of threats in new ideas, and those who are not afraid to swim outside the mainstream. Yes, the agent may become extinct, but only if he is the rigid, unthinking person who fails to take actions that will secure his future in the financial services industry.

Agents must now examine closely the strategies of all companies within the industry. They must identify the forward lookers, those who are reacting effectively and decisively to the financial services industry's changing complexities. Agents must look for and respond to companies that are attempting to work with, not against, agents to solve prospecting and servicing problems. And they must identify the dinosaurs—those companies whose hind legs are anchored firmly in the past. Now, I realize that my fellow executives might regard these comments as a kind of treason, but that's all right. Remember, they also said selling anything other than traditional whole life was treason.

The agents who survive the financial services revolution will be those who get their priorities straight. The successful agents of the future will be independent in their thinking and acting. They will recognize that one company cannot be all things to all people. With rapid changes in consumer attitudes and a proliferation of new products available, the agent must be in a position to offer many choices.

What agents must realize is that companies need them more than they need companies. Companies do their best to convince the agent it's the other way around, except that is not the case. The company cannot survive without the agent and it's about time agents took advantage of this position. By working together to demand products and marketing techniques more in line with the realities of today's world, agents can force the industry to grow with the shifting tides of the market.

I'm not opposed to loyalty; I'm just suggesting that loyalty should be given the old fashioned way—it should be earned. Agents should be just as loyal to companies as companies are to agents. The companies like to pass out a number of placebos, but agents should realize that actions really do speak louder than words.

One thing I've learned after 20 years of experience in the life insurance industry is that a company's definition of loyalty is usually limited to the amount of premium sold by an agent the previous week. Sometimes even that is not enough for some companies. As Bobby Anderson wrote, "The agent feels betrayed when he discovers that his home office attempts to bring about Internal Revenue Service rulings and/or legislation that would make less favorable to the public the Universal Life product, simply because it is not in the best interest of *his* home office to market such a product. Even less inspiring is the fact that simultaneously his home office is trying to purchase behind the scenes a smaller stock company through which it can market the Universal Life product, just in case the lobbying efforts are unsuccessful in blocking the product from the public and the agent."[2]

Companies go to great lengths and spend sizeable amounts of money trying to build the loyalty of the agent. Yet in return, the agent rarely receives lasting loyalty from the company. This situation was emphasized a few years ago when a *Fortune* 500 company decided to buy some large policies on their executives. They were initially sold on the concept by one of the insurance company's career agents, but when the prospect company went directly to the insurance company, the agent was directly eliminated.

In another situation, I was told of an agent who uncovered a prospect who was ready to implement a Retired Lives Reserve plan. When the agent went back to his company and asked for a proposal, he was told the company didn't offer the product. The company went so far as to tell the agent they didn't think RLR was a good sale. Later the agent found out his prospect had purchased the RLR plan from a national brokerage house—and the policies were issued by his loyal company.

One of the most blatant examples of the industry's double standard definition of loyalty is being demonstrated today by

Metropolitan Life. As one of the largest career agent companies, Metropolitan takes the position their agents can write only the company products—no brokerage. I've been told agents have been threatened with termination if they broker some business. Yet, at the same time, the company is in the midst of aggressively advertising for brokerage business. It seems it's okay for the company to play both sides of the fence, but the agents better not try it.

I'm not saying actions like these are right or wrong, but agents should recognize these attitudes and place their loyalty where it is deserved. Loyalty is very important for companies; they dwell on it. Probably the second most often used word in the home office vocabulary—behind premium—is loyalty.

A good example of this attitude was found in an article written by Kerry Grantham, vice president of Fidelity Union Life. In the article Mr. Grantham said, "The issue of loyalty has serious ramifications in our business. Both agents and managers need to remind themselves from time to time how important it is to maintain a supportive attitude toward the home office and the agency department." Mr. Grantham concludes the article with this admonition to the reader: "Support your company, your agent, your managers, your church, your family, your alma mater and your friends."[3] I found it interesting to note that not once in the article did the writer suggest the company has any obligation to be loyal to the agent. I love the order of loyalty picked by Mr. Grantham—company before all. Loyalty is fine, but loyalty must be a two-way street or it leads down the road to betrayal.

My experiences are probably typical of many agents recruited by career agency companies. I entered the life insurance business as a career agent for New England Mutual Life. Almost from the very first recruiting interview, I was drenched with propaganda about how wonderful New England Life was, and why I owed it to the company to be loyal. Early training stressed that the company and its products were so good I shouldn't even think about writing business with another company. The strategy worked. I was young, impressionable and, some might say, naive.

I remember the feeling of trauma when I left New England Life. I had spent five loyal years with the company and had fallen for all the bunk they offered. The company attempted to create the idea that if you weren't with an Eastern, mutual, New York company, you really were not in the life insurance business. I was loyal to the company and loyal to the image they tried to portray. Of course, if I had failed to produce a substantial amount of sales, I would be gone.

I went from an Eastern, mutual, general agency company to a Southern, stock, managerial company—Jefferson Standard Life. I was so hung up with the loyalty ideas of New England Life that when the Jefferson Standard recruiter approached me, I was almost embarrassed when we met for the interview. So successful had New England Life been at instilling loyalty that after joining Jefferson Standard, I stopped going to industry meetings for a while because I felt like a traitor.

One of the first things I discovered after my move was that Jefferson Standard also had good products. When I sold a policy, my hands did not get dirty; not only did I get paid in American money, I got more of it. In addition, I found the people I dealt with at Jefferson Standard were a lot more genuine than the people I had met at New England Life.

Even so, five years later when State Mutual offered me a job in its home office, I found that feeling of insurance tradition was still there. It was almost as if I were being offered the chance to get back into the "real" life insurance business. That feeling lasted for about two months.

There was the attitude at State Mutual, almost blatantly expressed, that the field force and the consumer existed only for the benefit of the company. After having been in the field as an agent and general agent for ten years, the first big shock I received after entering a home office was finding out that many company executives really didn't like the agents. I had been out in the field, heard all those great things uttered by home office executives, and believed just about all of it. What a shock to find out it was all a joke, part of a big game with the agents no more than production machines on a factory floor.

I realize these are harsh words but, unfortunately, they are true. There are a lot of people in home offices who are very loyal to agents, but they are the exception rather than the rule. Almost from the time I started working at State Mutual, I was involved in meetings designed to, in effect, gain tighter control of the agent. State Mutual operated under a general agency contract system but the management seemed convinced that the general agents had become too big and powerful. From the company's standpoint, the general agents had become too independent. State Mutual hired consultants, held myriads of meetings and spent hundreds of thousands of dollars—all with the objective of changing the general agents to managers.

Now, the company didn't need to hire all those consultants, hold boring meetings, and spend hundreds of thousands of dollars just to decide it wanted to be a managerial company. It appeared to me as if that decision had been made long before the first consultant was hired. Yet, it was necessary to do all that if you didn't want the general agents to know what you were doing.

Certainly State Mutual, or any other company, has the right to run the company any way it wants. I'm not criticizing that, or even the fact that companies may tell their field force one thing while they are doing another. Nor is it my intention to single out State Mutual as the only company with a questionable attitude toward their agents. Believe me, they are not alone. There are many very good people working at State Mutual and I like all of them, right down to the core. I've heard and seen much worse attitudes from other company executives at many Life Insurance Marketing and Research Association (LIMRA) and ACLI meetings. I raise this issue only to make sure agents are aware of this type of attitude and take steps to protect themselves. The fact that companies say one thing and then do another should not come as a surprise or disappointment to the sophisticated individual.

Well, if we can't count on companies to look out for the interests of agents, surely some of the national agent organizations can be relied on to take up the slack. An organization that calls itself the National Association of Life Underwriters certainly sounds like it should have the best interests of the agent at heart. With membership over 130,000 and annual dues exceeding $10,000,000 the NALU and its various state and local associations should be a very strong voice for the interests of the agents. Here is another situation where logic would lead you to such a conclusion but, again, you would be wrong.

It may not have been a conscious decision, but I believe the NALU, created to support the agents has, for the most part, deserted them. Positions taken by the Million Dollar Round Table (MDRT), the American Society of CLU, and the General Agents and Managers Association (GAMA) have not done much to help agents either but, to be fair, their role is really not the same as the NALU.

It's disappointing to see that so many national leaders of agent organizations either cannot, or will not, recognize the hypocrisy of many companies. What is worse, these people seem to have been seduced by and sing the siren of the companies rather than the song of the agents. Almost always, the NALU and other agent organizations take the same position on issues as do the companies and their industry organization, the American Council of Life Insurance (ACLI).

Can any reasonable person believe that the interests of the companies and the interests of the agents are always in harmony? Come now. Can you think of one critical issue—any issue—on which the National Association of Life Underwriters has disagreed with an industry position espoused by the American Council of Life Insurance?

Back in 1981, when the companies were quietly trying to stem the tide of policyholder loans by seeking legislation to raise the loan interest rate, the initial reaction of many local life underwriter chapters was to oppose the change. Some members felt raising loan interest rates was not in the best interest of their clients. However, it was in the financial interests of the companies and so the NALU quickly agreed and supported the companies. Earlier that year, I remember attending an exclusive, and not well-publicized, Executive Round Table of the ACLI in Florida. At the meetings (between the rounds of golf) a number of CEOs got up and told us how they had met with the leaders of the NALU and "encouraged" them to support the loan interest package. Just to cover all the bases, they instructed us on how to pressure our agents to lobby their local Life Underwriter Associations to support the companies' position on policy loans. We were even given copies of letters or bulletins that we were instructed to send to the agents.

Another issue where the NALU seems to have been led along by the ACLI is unisex. Why on earth the NALU should use the hard earned dollars of field agents to fight unisex is beyond me. The companies argued that unisex rates would put them out of business. Hogwash! Retroactive unisex rates maybe, but the government had agreed not to push for retroactivity if the companies would use unisex on a going-forward basis.

The companies opposed unisex rates, not because it would be any great catastrophe, but because it was a change. The industry had all the actuarial arguments, but what they didn't realize was that unisex was not an actuarial question, but a social one. Sure, the actuarial tables say women live longer and because of this the industry argued women should be charged a different rate for their insurance. Still, actuarial tables show that people in Utah live longer than people in Mississippi, and that blacks have a higher mortality rate than whites. Why doesn't the industry charge different rates to these groups? They used to. Obviously, different rates can't and shouldn't be charged for blacks and whites because it would not be socially, or legally, acceptable.

Unisex rates would have virtually no impact on the life insurance industry—except to make the policies for men a little more competitive. By appearing to blindly follow the lead of the ACLI, the NALU and its members are made to look out-of-step with the times and over 50 percent of the consumers.

If the NALU's only objective is to protect and support agents, why does *Life Association News* refuse to accept ads that specifically discuss commissions? Ask yourself, "Who does this rule protect, the companies or the agents? Why would the NALU seek to protect the companies rather than make competitive information available to agents?" Could the answer be money? I'll let you draw your own conclusions.

The American Council of Life Insurance has indicated opposition to the entrance of banks into the life insurance business. The leaders of the NALU tag along as if being pulled by a ring through their nose. Nearly every month there are stories in *Life Association News* about the horrible vandal bankers that will sweep down out of the north to rape, pillage, and burn the village of life insurance. Later, I'll address the issue of banks in life insurance and why this is another example of how companies sometimes speak with a forked-tongue. Just let me ask you this: Do life insurance agents, the best salespeople in existence, really need to be afraid of organizations where sophisticated marketing is defined as giving out toaster ovens?

I think agent organizations should represent agents to the industry, not the industry to the agents. Testifying before Congress about reducing taxes is great for the ego, but how about talking a little more about companies that are trying to reduce the number of agents? I believe the national leaders of organizations like the National Association of Life Underwriters have lost touch with their membership; and I'm not the only one to feel that way. I find the local leaders and members are very much in touch with what is happening in a changing financial world. When I speak before local life underwriters associations that have the courage to hear me, there are two consistent comments: first, the program chairperson invariably tells me, "This is the largest turnout we have had in years." Second, members come up after the meeting and say, "I heard all the bad things about you and came here to argue with you and your ideas. But after listening, I find I'm in almost full agreement." It's apparent from the reaction I get that the agents have not lost touch with the real world. I'm not sure the same can be said for many agent leaders.

This is not a time for agents to be deserted by people who are actually being paid to fight for them. When you stop to think about the situation, it's really not surprising that the NALU, more often than not, takes positions that favor the companies over the agent. After all, the NALU is being heavily subsidized by the companies. In the name of professionalism, many companies virtually require agents to join the NALU. By forcing those who might not otherwise do so, the companies are, in effect, subsidizing the NALU.

A more subtle form of this coercion to join the NALU is tied to agent recognition. Most companies make a big deal about the Million Dollar Round Table membership and the National Quality Award. Since key awards such as these require NALU membership, more money is poured into the coffers of the NALU. Now, do you think the companies would take actions like this if they felt the NALU was going to take positions contrary to those of the companies? And don't think the national leaders of the NALU, especially the salaried ones, don't recognize this financial reality.

I know of no other major industry where "management" virtually requires the "workers" to join a worker association. Imagine a baseball owner calling one of his bright rookie prospects to his office and saying, "Zeke, I really like the way you're playing. You're off to a great start and have a bright future in this game."

"Gee, thanks, Mr. Megabucks. I'm givin' 110 percent all out for the team."

"Oh, Zeke, there is one thing. I notice here that you haven't joined the Players' Association."

"Well, you know, Mr. Megabucks, all I want to do is play baseball."

"Yes, but Zeke, all real ballplayers join the association. And besides, you can't make the All-Star team, get a Gold Glove for quality play or win the MVP unless you belong to the Players' Association. You want those awards, don't you?"

"Sure, Mr. Megabucks, but. . ."

"But what?"

"Well, you see, Mr. Megabucks, you know, I'm on minimum salary. You said I'd appreciate my success a lot more if I sacrificed when I'm getting started. . .and, so you see, I really don't have the money for the dues."

"Hey, no problem, Zeke, what are we here for if we can't help our players. We'll pay the dues and then take them out of your next three checks."

"Gee, thanks, Mr. Megabucks."

"Okay, Zeke, you just get out there and build your career. Oh, one more thing, just make sure you go to all those Association meetings."

Now, for obvious reasons, it's hard to imagine a conversation like that at the ballpark. The Baseball Players Association has not lost sight of, nor has it stopped fighting for, the rights of its members. Still, similar conversations have been held thousands of times in agencies all around the country.

The National Association of Life Underwriters, which started out with grand enthusiasm and purpose, today serves a very important role for the companies. As the policy loan interest rate situation demonstrated, a supposedly independent agent organization gave dues paying agent members the exact line they heard from the companies. What is the agent to believe if he hears one thing from his company and then goes to his association meeting to hear the same story? If the national leaders of the NALU want this organization to be a megaphone for the companies, that's fine. The only point I'm trying to make is that agents should be aware of where the NALU's financial loyalty lies and act accordingly.

Today, I know of only one organization that really speaks for the agent. It's a small group called The American Council of

Independent Life Underwriters (ACILU). This group, led by Charlie Dyer, is concerned only about one thing—the survival of the agent. It has the same fervor that the NALU had at its founding, but somehow lost. Of course, the industry's reaction to a group like the ACILU has been swift and negative.

Life Association News refused, without explanation, to accept ads from the ACILU. The NALU also refused to let the ACILU rent exhibition space at its 1983 annual convention. Both these actions were taken despite the fact that Charlie Dyer goes out of his way to point out that he believes the NALU performs a valuable service, and does not view the new organization as a countermovement. Mr. Dyer views his role primarily as an educator of agent rights. You'd think the NALU and the other so-called agent organizations would welcome some additional support.

That is not the case, however. In fact, at least one other organization, the Million Dollar Round Table, has jumped up to support the NALU in its resistance to this new organization. In a letter written on March 10, 1983, MDRT executive vice president, Roderick L. Geer, CLU, expressed the following point of view: "We are aware of the article which appeared in the *National Underwriter* describing the American Council of Independent Life Underwriters in Pensacola, Florida. In fact, I discussed the matter with Jack Bobo and John Driskill of our sister associations, NALU and ASCLU, just this past week.

"Simply stated, the Million Dollar Round Table has no position with respect to this new organization, nor do I see any particular reason why we should. It is comprised of a relatively small number of producers who appear to operate largely on a brokerage basis and have few, if any, company loyalties. Candidly, I am very surprised that the *National Underwriter* bothered to give this organization the credibility of a major column on page two of their February 5th edition. It would seem to me that they are contributing little but confusion to the insurance scene—and falsely testifying that agents are getting 'half-truths' from their companies and associations. I don't believe that is true of any of the companies or associations with which I am familiar—and I am positive it is untrue as it relates to MDRT.

"Fortunately for all of us, professional life underwriters in this country have a choice—a choice of belonging to the 140 or so members of ACILU—or the 140,000 members of NALU. Hopefully, we will all choose to deal from strength and experience, as well as time-tested professionalism."

Well, excuse me! This letter appears to be a classic example of just how paranoid and arrogant some leaders of agent organizations have become. Let's examine this letter and see what we can learn.

First of all, we see how sensitive and fearful these organizations are when a single article in the *National Underwriter*[4] about an organization with 140 members forces the "sister associations" into a quick powwow. What is it these people fear? Will agents learn something these "sister associations" don't want them to know? Mr. Geer says the MDRT "has no position with respect to this new organization" and then, as the MDRT's executive vice president, goes on to "candidly" attack the ACILU. He was "very surprised that the *National Underwriter* bothered to" write about this new organization. (A copy of the letter was sent to the *National Underwriter.*) Why would the writer be surprised? Does he feel the "sister associations" are the only ones who should get coverage? If you're really doing such a good job for your members, a little publicity for another organization should not be cause for alarm.

In the letter, Mr. Geer is concerned about the ACILU because its members "have few, if any, company loyalties." Here we are with that thing about loyalty to companies. Is blind company loyalty a requirement for a professional agent? Are agents who qualify for the MDRT by writing business with more than one company not really "true members"? Is there something wrong with people who broker business? There are many companies that don't like brokers, but why should the "independent" MDRT worry about company loyalty?

Mr. Geer worries that the ACILU is ". . .contributing little but confusion to the insurance scene. . ." It appears that any viewpoint not following the party line of the "sister associations" causes confusion. Confusion for whom; the agents, or the organizations that seem to want the agents to hear only one story? In an industry with over 250,000 members, why is there no room for divergent points of view?

Mr. Geer seems upset because the ACILU intimates that sometimes the companies and associations are not always fully candid with agents. He doesn't know of any companies or associations where this has been the case. Where has he been? With these "sister associations" seeming to want agents to receive only one approved line of information, one of the first things agents ought to do to start the fight to survive would be to support organizations like the ACILU.

I've personally experienced the same reaction from the "sister associations." Four years ago, when I went public about the competitiveness, or lack thereof, of the products being offered by the industry, the NALU was the first to brand me as anti-insurance and anti-agent. Little did it matter that the consumer was actually saying worse things about traditional whole life. I felt that if our industry did not begin to offer better products, our credibility with the consumer would continue to sink. I felt the future, not only of the agent but the industry as well, was at stake. I said the fault was with the companies, not the agents, who were as much a victim as the consumer. It was the NALU who then took up the defense for the companies.

As I traveled around the country, I offered to present my views on the life insurance industry before various local life underwriter associations. Due to the attacks from the NALU, I initially received a nearly unanimous chorus of "no" to my offer. Many who did schedule an appearance later called to cancel. One local group canceled just the day before my appearance and said, "It was decided your ideas would be too dangerous for new agents to hear." I had a number of program chairmen tell me they had received "a lot of pressure from Washington" to cancel my appearance.

As the times changed, however, and the newer products were being introduced, a few of the local life underwriter associations began offering invitations. Of course, the early meetings usually required me to debate an actuary because everyone thought we were arguing about products. People still did not realize that a debate about products was a debate over the symptoms of an illness, not over the cure.

Today, in one respect, the story is quite a bit different. I have been fortunate to receive many invitations from the progressive, open, local associations and, as I have mentioned before, we have had some great meetings. I have been proud to receive letters saying, "Your presentation was the best meeting we have ever had." Of course, not everyone agrees with my point of view, but that's not the point.

Yet, this has still not stopped the NALU from trying to prevent my appearance before local chapters. I've been told of a memo that went out from Washington suggesting that only those programs following the approved party line should be scheduled. Even today, there are still many local associations that fear having their members exposed to viewpoints that do not have the industry imprimatur. Fortunately for all of us in life insurance, this attitude is moving from the majority to the minority.

Local leaders and agents are responding to our challenges in a positive way, but the NALU seems even more entwined with the interests of the companies and the beliefs of the past. Demonstration of this continuing attitude was best expressed by a member of the NALU board of trustees who said in a speech, "Mr. MacDonald has challenged me to debate with him about the future of the life insurance industry . . . I have no interest whatever in Mr. MacDonald's views on the future of the life insurance industry. And considering Mr. MacDonald's record of accomplishments in the life industry, someone interested in a bright future in the life insurance industry might do well to find out what Mr. MacDonald is doing and do the exact opposite."[5] Some may not want to face the future, and that's their problem, but what about those agents who do care? Chances are, agents who dare to be independent and different will continue to be attacked by traditionalists. Those with the courage to take the driver's seat on a road less traveled, those who are willing to explore non-traditional ideas, those who don't accept the first or easiest answer, will be the ones to survive and emerge into a prosperous future.

Despite what many are saying and more are thinking, the future holds tremendous opportunity for the truly professional life underwriter. The agent who is independent, honest, competent and attempts to offer a competitive, balanced financial plan will not only survive, but thrive. Today the agent stands poised at a critical point in the history of our industry. He or she must make some choices. Agents can allow themselves to be led by those who seek only pat answers, those unwilling to consider ideas that don't have the industry stamp of approval, and stumble into a mysterious future determined by the companies and those they control. Or, agents can take control of their destiny and move ahead with open eyes and cool confidence, prepared to explore all alternatives and clear the obstacles that await them.

Unfortunately, many agents are going to sit and watch what the future brings. On the contrary, I think agents can do better than that. Agents are smarter than the "sister associations" and their "loyal" companies think. Agents can, must, and will stand up to assure their survival and as a result, create a positive future. If they don't care . . . no one else will!

Chapter III Notes

[1] Bobby D. Anderson, CLU, "Who Cares About the Agent?" *Life Insurance Selling,* February 1982.

[2] *Ibid.*

[3] Kerry J. Grantham, CLU, "Loyalty Makes the System Work for You," *Life Association News,* May 1984, p. 82.

[4] Ian MacKenzie, "New Agent Association is Talking Tough!" *National Underwriter,* Life and Health edition, February 5, 1983, pp. 5, 20.

[5] Alan Press, speech before the Minnesota Association of Life Underwriters, April 26, 1985.

4

COLLECTING PREMIUMS INSTEAD OF GIVING THEM

In the last few years, those of us in the life insurance industry have been concerned about many issues—taxation, unisex, product development—but one overriding emotional issue has dominated much of our thought and discussion. That issue is the question of banks entering the insurance business. Emotion on both sides has run rampant, and the discussion of bank deregulation has turned into a battle of Armageddon proportions between the two giant industries of financial services—insurance and banking. The life insurance and banking industries have been on a virtual war footing. It is a war without trumpets or drums, without artillery or B-52s; but it has not been a silent war.

Banks have been under tremendous competitive pressure in their industry and see the insurance industry as greener pastures. In an effort to develop much needed new profit centers, banks have been trying to scale the barriers that keep them from selling insurance. Insurance executives, already reeling from product changes and challenged by an antiquated distribution system, are trying to protect their turf. In doing this they have rolled up their lobbying artillery in Washington and elsewhere hoping to keep banks out of the village of life insurance. Insurance executives have set up barbed wire everywhere they can. They figure their survival and prosperity hinge on keeping the hordes of bankers from scaling the village walls.

The irony in all this activity is that each industry is strong in exactly the area where the other is weak. Each one is a mirror image of the other. The banking industry has a massive distribution system that needs to improve its marketing expertise. The life insurance industry excels in marketing techniques, but needs to improve its distribution system. For everyone's benefit, it's time for this war to stop. I'm not proposing that the hot war simply cool down to a cold war, or become an armed truce with the two sides glaring at each other. Nor am I simply proposing a bilateral freeze. I do want to wage peace, but what I propose is even more radical.

I believe it's time for banks and the insurance industry to begin working together as partners, not rivals. It's time to merge the strengths of these industries into a strong alliance—a partnership that will help overcome the respective weaknesses in both industries and provide each with the opportunity to grow and prosper. And, I might add, this prosperity will not come at the expense of the consumer. On the contrary, I believe a partnership between banks and the insurance industry will benefit the consumer in the form of better products and improved, more convenient service.

Now, I acknowledge that as far as agents are concerned, I have a tough sale ahead of me. Agents, who have been the infantry in this war, have been filled with visions of what will happen to them and to the noncombatants (the consumer) if they lose this war and are captured by the banks.

The industry propaganda machines seem to want the agents to believe they will be wiped out. Listening to the screeds against banks selling insurance, one might come to believe the consumer will be raped, pillaged and, worst of all, shamelessly coerced by those evil and devious bankers. As a result, many agents have been leading the fight against banks. This is a very myopic approach to the realities and opportunities available. Actually, agents should be leading the fight to get banks into the insurance business.

Banks can play a key role in the salvation of the agent because they can perform a task most agents find both difficult and onerous—prospecting. Banks can help agents solve the productivity problem by bringing the prospect to the agent, and allowing the agent to do what he does best—sell.

I don't believe anyone suggests that banks will be the total answer to the distribution challenges faced by the agency system. If, however, agents are going to win this battle for survival, joining forces with the banks is just one tactic that we cannot afford to reject just because it's new and different. Working with banks should not be rejected out-of-hand simply because industry leaders tell us it's a bad idea, that is, except when they want to do it. The discussion of banks in the insurance industry is a major part of the distribution issue and should be approached from an unemotional and logical perspective.

In an effort to do this, I'm going to divide this chapter into a series of independent sections. In these sections, we will explore why banks want to get into insurance, if they do; closely examine the insurance industry's arguments against bank entrance into insurance; and review what some feel is a double standard insurance companies use when dealing with banks and agents. In the next chapter, I'll offer some reasons why I believe agents should be working with, not against, banks and suggest some steps agents can take to develop relationships with banks and other financial institutions.

As we explore the banking question, consider the following point of view expressed by Donald T. Regan, then Secretary of the Treasury and now Presidential Chief of Staff: ". . . the question is not *whether* bank-affiliated organizations will be able to offer insurance. . . but *how*." He went on, "If the insurance in-

industry does nothing but oppose change, it risks being left out of the debate on the direction of change—but it won't stop change."[1]

The Changing Banking Industry

If you think we in the insurance business have gone through some revolutionary traumas, well, it's nothing compared to what the bankers have been experiencing. There is an old joke dealing with how banks are managed. It's called the 3-6-3 rule of banking. Under this rule, bankers are said to pay three percent interest on deposits, charge six percent interest on loans, and be on the golf course by three o'clock.

As with most humor, the truth is not far below the surface. The modern American banking industry was built in an atmosphere of heavy regulation and supervision. The regulations were imposed after the depression of the 1930s primarily as a protection for the consumer, but also to restore confidence in the banking system. The objectives were achieved but, unfortunately, at the expense of competition.

By regulation, banks were prevented from competing in the market sensitive segments of their industry which is how much interest they pay to get money, and how much they charge to give out money. Since it was government policy to virtually assure that banks were profitable, expenses associated with running a bank could be easily passed along to the consumer. With no difference in the products offered, there was a sameness in the industry, and individual banks began searching for some way to differentiate themselves from the "competition" across the street. The answer most bankers hit upon was to begin offering a wide variety of consumer services at, what appeared to be little, if any, direct cost to the consumer.

First, we saw the advent of extended banking hours. It wasn't very long ago that normal banking hours ran from 10:00 a.m.

to 3:00 p.m., five days a week. (Maybe the 3-6-3 rule was no joke!) After expanded banking hours came free checking accounts, free travelers checks, free deposit boxes, and that great invention of the banking industry—the toaster oven. It got to the point where banks were giving out more premiums than Prudential was collecting.

Banks prided themselves on personal service, and lots of it. It did not matter if the services were cost inefficient because the expenses could be passed along without impacting the bottom line. Banks did very well under this system but then along came inflation and with it high interest rates. These rates were offered by non-banking instruments such as cash management accounts, money market funds, government securities, and single premium deferred annuities. As opposed to bank products, none of these interest sensitive products were controlled by the government. When consumers saw inflation rates of five, eight and even 18 percent eat away, not only at the interest credited on bank savings but at the principal itself, they began taking money out of banks in bushel baskets.

Money market funds went from an unknown quantity to over $200 billion in assets in just a few short years. That's $0.00 to $200,000,000,000.00 almost overnight. Most of that money came right out of bank accounts and, because of the regulations that had previously protected them, the bankers were powerless to stop the outflow. (Also, because the life insurance industry was experiencing the same disintermediation problems, we know a few billion of those money market funds came out of whole life policies. The only difference was, no government regulation prevented insurance companies from offering a more competitive product.)

The banks responded by claiming the financial services playing field was not level, that it was tilted against them. The walls that served so well as protection against competition suddenly became their prison. Bankers began lobbying hard to have their interest sensitive products deregulated. Sometimes you have to be careful what you wish for because you may get it. Regulation

Q, which controlled the amount of interest banks could pay on small savings accounts, was repealed and suddenly banks were free to compete in the open market for the consumers' saving dollar. The only problem was that they were not ready. Most bankers, especially the regional and community banks, did not know how to compete. If the consumer has the choice between ten percent interest or three percent interest and a toaster, which do you think they will choose?

The local and regional banks were at a particular disadvantage in this situation. In order to maintain their deposit base, local institutions found themselves having to offer very high rates of interest and still provide many of their "free" services. Suddenly, all those tellers, free checking accounts and beautiful bank offices became very expensive. The automatic, built-in profit margins disappeared. If the banks charged the needed fees, the consumers could become upset and take their money elsewhere. If the banks covered the cost of the services, they couldn't afford to pay the competitive rates of interest needed to attract money. The national institutions were not looked to for these services and, therefore, were in the position of being able to come into a local market, offer high rates of interest, and "scoop the cream" off the top. In order to remain profitable, in fact for survival, the bankers caught in this squeeze were forced to start looking for additional ways to develop income. Since it was a financial vehicle, it was logical that banks would look to insurance as a potential new profit center.

What is ironic about the life insurance industry's battle to keep banks out of insurance is the fact that most bankers don't want to get into insurance. Many feel they are being forced into insurance as a matter of survival. Some of the large institutions like CitiBank, Bank of America and First Interstate are moving aggressively, but most of the 15,000 banks are not large and feel they are simply being pulled along.

During the last few years, I've had the opportunity to talk before a number of banking organizations. The strongest impression I get is that bankers just want to be bankers. They do not want to be in the insurance business. However, they are trying to survive, and to do that, they need new profit centers. Insurance looks like a good option but it certainly has not been singled out as the business banks must enter. Banks are also exploring discount brokerage, leasing services and, believe it or not, travel agency services.

Sometimes those of us in the insurance business get so paranoid we think everyone is picking on us. Banks don't care if they get into the insurance business, they just need some additional ways of making money. Many in the life insurance industry view banks as a threat, but there are others who see opportunity and will take advantage of it.

At meetings where I have made this point, some agents have come up to me and said, "If the bankers got themselves into this situation, why should we be the ones to suffer? Why don't we just let them stew, and keep making those South American loans?" Normally, I might be convinced to agree with this logic. Yet just as we have something to offer banks, they have something to offer us. Banks need a new profit center and insurance can provide the answer. The life insurance industry needs an efficient way to reach prospects and banks can provide the answer.

Keep the Heathens Out

The life insurance industry does not like competition of any sort, and has responded to the encroachment of banks on its turf as if some horrible plague were spreading across the life insurance industry. The players go running to mother (government) saying, "Hey, they broke their wagon and want to play with ours. You can't let them do that, or they'll break our wagon, too." To me, it's interesting irony that the life insurance industry fights hard to prevent federal regulation of insurance, but when a state (South Dakota) allows banks to sell insurance, the industry asks Congress for federal legislation to block such action.

The basic arguments raised by the industry to keep the banks out of insurance boil down to these three categories: 1) Bankers don't know how to underwrite insurance and will have to use funds from bank accounts to pay claims; 2) banks will eliminate the need for agents and; 3) banks will use their financial position as lender and seller to unfairly coerce customers into buying insurance products they don't want or need.

As far as I'm concerned, all of these arguments are pure smoke and have no validity. If the insurance industry were to argue that bankers should not be allowed to sell insurance because they are not smart enough—that they'd all fail the AIB test—then I might agree. But the arguments raised are spurious, at best. I also believe the industry leaders know the arguments are not valid but use them to further their own ends. Let's now address each of these arguments.

The first point made by many critics of banks in insurance is that bankers don't know how to underwrite insurance and will do it all wrong. This argument would lead one to believe that every bank in the country is going to go out and buy or start an insurance company. Of course, bankers don't know how to underwrite insurance. (If you look at the underwriting results of the property and casualty industry during the last few years, one might wonder if there are any insurance people who know how to underwrite insurance.) The fact is, most bankers do not want to, and never will underwrite insurance.

Today there are approximately 15,000 banks doing business in the United States. Of that number 10, or maybe 15, are large enough or interested enough to want to have their own manufacturing plant for insurance. Even if you say 100 banks want to own a life insurance company, that still leaves 14,900 banks that will simply be distributors of insurance. They will have no say in the underwriting of the policies. Of those banks that eventually end up owning a life insurance company, are we to believe the loan officer or chief teller will suddenly be named chief underwriter or chief actuary? Of course not, bank holding companies that own life insurance companies will do just what every other company owning an insurance company does, and that's hire insurance people to run the company.

The experience of financial institutions distributing insurance has been reasonably good, but the record of ownership has been poor. Financial institutions that have purchased life insurance companies have usually paid much more than the company was worth and then were not able to make it successful. Banks will be good distributors, but they will be no threat as underwriters or direct competitors.

The other part of the underwriting argument says that when banks get into trouble they will "mix and match" the insurance assets with those of the banks. Even the insurance company executives who use this argument have to suppress a smirk when they raise it. If anything, the double regulation that's involved in both banking and insurance will stop companies from taking any action, let alone mixing assets. Let's remember that the deregulation we are talking about has to do only with involvement in insurance. We are not talking about taking all supervisory regulations away and letting banks and insurance companies do anything they wish.

Most people raising this "mixing of assets" argument like to cite Baldwin-United as an example of what will happen if banks are allowed to enter insurance. This makes a nice story, but what does it have to do with banks? Baldwin was a piano company. I believe the supervisory regulations for banking are a bit more strict than those for piano companies. The Baldwin-United fiasco might never have happened if the company had been a bank.

The second big point raised against banks entering the insurance industry argues that banks would eliminate the agent and service to the consumer would suffer. Let me tell you one thing: I've been dealing with bankers for about three years and I can promise you, they are no threat to the survival of the agent. Bankers are absolutely the worst sales and marketing people in existence today. It may be hard to believe, but they rank well behind underwriters and actuaries when it comes to selling.

A banker's marketing philosophy is the exact opposite of the life insurance industry's. Bankers know that people will come to them to borrow money and, as a result, have developed a very passive marketing attitude. Most bankers define marketing as full-page ads in the local newspaper, some tent cards in the lobby, a few statement stuffers, and sitting back to wait for the phone to ring. We know this style of "marketing" will not work when it comes to selling insurance. To repeat the old, but true, cliche: "Insurance is sold, not bought." As a result of this, the insurance industry has always used an intrusive marketing approach.

Think about the times you have gone into a bank and there in the lobby you see a dusty rack with a lot of little pamphlets outlining the various services offered by the bank. How many times has someone in the bank come up to you and said, "Do you have a couple of minutes? I've got an idea that may be of value to you." Why do you think bankers opted for discount brokerage rather than full-service? It's because they view themselves as running a service and not a sales organization. This attitude goes back to the days of full regulation, and the bankers have not changed. I can assure you, the good life insurance agent has little to fear from the teller, trust or loan officer when it comes to selling insurance. I smile every time I go into my local bank to make a loan and the loan officer says, "Now, you don't want credit insurance do you?" To him, the credit sale does not mean more money for the bank but an extra form to fill out. He sees his job as making the loan, not selling the insurance.

Insurance will not become a major profit center for banks unless they are working very closely with professional agents. Most bankers I know admit this point. They'll try direct mail and sell some cancer policies because that's passive and easy, but do you want to sell that sort of policy anyway? When it comes to real insurance, banks will not eliminate the need for the agent. On the contrary, banks will create an increased need for good, professional agents.

The last major area of fear raised by insurance people against banks in insurance involves the undue influence banks could exert over the consumer because they have full financial information and have power as a money lender. John Creedon, president of

Metropolitan, raised this issue in testimony before Congress on May 29, 1984, when he said, "Of particular concern is the possible undue influence that might be exerted upon a prospective borrower—whether individual or business—to purchase insurance through the lending institution. The obvious evil is that the consumer's purchase decision will be based not on the price or quality of the insurance product, but on the consumer's perceived need to please the extender of credit and to show that he is a 'full service' customer worthy of being granted a loan."[2]

It is obvious from the above testimony that Mr. Creedon believes that it is not proper to be both lender and insurance seller. I will admit that the possibility for abuse does exist in this area, but I don't believe it to be a major problem. The current Truth-in-Lending legislation already prohibits such activity; even that could be supplemented by specific laws to make such activity illegal and impose stiff penalties for violation. Now, I'm not naive enough to believe that legislation alone will eliminate a potential abuse. . . greed is greed. There will be situations where individuals will take advantage of their power as an extender of credit, but I don't believe that is sufficient reason to prejudge and eliminate everyone in the banking profession.

There is one other point to consider when discussing the issue of credit leverage and that is the matter of priorities. A banker's primary concern is to be a banker, not an insurance person. Bankers are seeking to make money selling insurance, but they still view their primary objectives to be building deposits and expanding their customer base so they can offer more bank services. If a banker makes a loan to someone and then coerces that person into buying insurance, the banker knows the customer will probably go to another bank the next time there is a need for a loan. Bankers view the sale of insurance as a way to attract more people to the banking services, not drive them away.

Savings banks and thrifts have been allowed to sell insurance for many years, and to the best of my knowledge, there has never been one example of people being systematically coerced by a bank or thrift into buying insurance in order to get a loan.

I might expect the coercion question to have more validity, and possibly be a problem, if an insurance company owned a bank or was a lender. In such a situation the objective of the company making the loan would be different, it would be to sell insurance.

This takes me back to Mr. Creedon's dire warnings to Congress. *The Wall Street Journal* had an interesting story about Metropolitan Life buying the Century 21 real estate company. The article said in part: "Mr. Maurer of Metropolitan Life said Century 21 will round the company's array of financial services companies. In the past 18 months, Metropolitan has acquired CrossLand Capital Corp. and Met-First Financial Co., both of which originate and service mortgages.

"Ideally," Mr. Maurer said, "a person who buys a home through Century 21 could, for example, also arrange for a mortgage through CrossLand. At the same time, the person could take care of his insurance and investment needs. Our plan in the years ahead is to have (Century 21) people market our products: mortgages, homeowners' insurance, annuities, everything we have available."[3]

Interesting! It seems some of our friends feel it's very wrong for banks to make loans and sell insurance, but for some reason, it's simply good business for insurance companies to make loans and sell insurance. (What is that old story about people in glass houses?)

Are Insurance Companies Really Against Banks Selling Insurance?

If one had spent any amount of time in the last few years attending insurance meetings or reading industry publications, one could very easily reach the conclusion that the life insurance companies are dead set against banks entering insurance. That individual would be wrong. Banks in insurance is just one more example of where companies have been less than candid with agents. It's certainly a situation of, "Do as I say, not as I do."

We are also presented with another instance of the NALU supporting company positions at the expense of the dues paying agent. Nearly each month *Life Association News* has articles telling agents of the dangers presented by the banking industry. All the articles have been one-sided and paint a picture of agent and industry destruction if banks are allowed to distribute insurance. It's hard to imagine that an issue like this is so black and white, but you would certainly get that impression reading the pages of *Life Association News.*

Insurance companies, on the other hand, are not treating the issue so cleanly. Sure, with one hand the insurance companies are encouraging agents to fight bank entrance into insurance. Do you know what they are doing with the other hand? They are out signing deals with banks.

In May of 1984, an issue of *Best's Management Reports* led with a headline that read, "Metropolitan's Creedon Criticizes Banks as Insurers."[4] Mr. Creedon is quoted as saying, "Congress should reinforce the doctrine of separation of banking from other lines of commerce by plugging the loopholes which permit. . . the states to include, within the definition of banking, insurance activities and other traditionally non-banking functions." Obviously, the management of Metropolitan Life is against banks distributing life insurance. Or are they? On September 20, 1984 a headline in *The Journal of Commerce* read, "Metropolitan to Sell Insurance in Mo. (Missouri) Banks."[5]

The Life Insurance and Marketing Research Association in a survey of 137 member companies, found that 36 had joint marketing ventures with banks. Ernest E. Cragg, president of LIMRA, was quoted in *The Journal of Commerce* as saying, "There won't be a big rush to the financial institutions, there will be a gradual buildup over the coming years." The article continued, "The LIMRA leader chose not to predict how many insurers would link with the financial institutions in the future, but suggested that more are expected to do so because those that currently have a relationship with a financial institution can see the fruits of their efforts in the form of increased sales."[6] Pardon my confusion here, but are we, or are we not, supposed to be against banks getting into insurance? I hear what companies are saying, but I can see what they are doing!

There is another side to this story. Have you noticed that a number of insurance companies—Prudential and Travelers to name a couple—are trying to, or have already purchased banks? Now, wait just a minute! If these companies really believe the banking and insurance industries should go their separate ways, how can they justify buying banks?

In a number of states around the country, the NALU and other agent organizations have filed suits attempting to block bank entrance into insurance. Have you ever read about an insurance company or the American Council of Life Insurance having filed or even joined in such a lawsuit? There may be some, but I haven't seen any!

As usual, the company executives all say the "right" things for publication, but when it comes down to getting in the trenches and really doing battle, where are they? As we said before, they're too busy making deals with banks to get involved. It seems they'd much rather have their favorite organization—the NALU—out leading the agents and spending the hard earned dues. This attitude is best explained in a *National Underwriter* article reporting on the American Bankers Association's National Insurance and Protection Conference of Financial Institutions. The following statement was attributed to an insurance company spokesman who responded to a question "with the understanding that he wouldn't be identified." This brave soul told the bankers, "But we recognize the facts as you all do: that you're heading more into deregulation. We're not sitting there pretending that our only interest is traditional whole life insurance and group insurance. We're coming more into other financial services. We are prepared to experiment with anybody in any major type of new and interesting endeavor offering fire insurance, homeowners insurance and many other types of programs. The hesitancy we had a year or two ago we do not have today."[7]

Why is it okay for companies to experiment with new and interesting endeavors, but agents are encouraged to fight and file suit against the same thing? Now don't get me wrong, I don't think it's a bad idea for insurance companies to make deals with banks to sell insurance; I think it's a good idea. The point I'm trying to make is that companies are once again not dealing in good faith when it comes to the agents.

Why would companies say one thing—encourage agents to take action to support their stated intention—and then do just the opposite? I think there are a number of reasons.

Initially, companies probably did view banks as a threat. Later, when they discovered the arrangement would not be so bad, or recognized that it was bound to happen, they didn't want to admit to the agents that the home office was wrong. In the history of life insurance, no home office has ever made a mistake!

Second, some companies may view the opportunity to work with banks as a chance to sell insurance without using the agent. They could see all those bank customers and had visions of agentless mass marketing programs dancing in their dreams. The best way to keep the agents out of the deal was to have them fighting the banks.

Two recent developments may underscore this point. In late 1985 the management of New England Life announced they had entered into a joint venture arrangement with First Interstate Bancorp to sell life insurance to the bank's customers. Thousands of loyal New England agents noted (or should have) that the report quietly mentioned "direct mail" as the primary means of marketing.[8]

Then in January, 1986 the *National Underwriter* reported that Metropolitan Life had inked a deal with an Arkansas savings and loan to open insurance centers in several of the thrift's branches. Of news to agents was the fact "that salaried sales reps will staff the insurance centers, rather than agents from Met's own sales force."[9]

Finally, and possibly the most logical reason, may be the fact that companies do not want agents making direct deals with banks. As we've seen, companies dwell on agent loyalty primarily so they can maintain control of the agent. If the agent makes a distribution deal with a bank, the companies fear loyalty will be shifted either to the bank providing the leads or (fear of fears) the consumer.

By encouraging agents to fight banks, the insurance companies are free to go out and make the distribution arrangements themselves. Then, when the agents are eventually brought in, as they will have to be, the companies not only maintain control, they set themselves up as "heroes" for finding a new way for the agent to prospect. One thing is clear, banks will eventually be allowed to distribute insurance. How agents react to this situation will determine how they participate in the final arrangement.

Chapter IV Notes

[1] Stephen Piontek, "Regan Seeks Industry Support For Dereg Bill," *National Underwriter*, Life and Health edition, November 26, 1983, p. 6.

[2] Al Goldsmith, "Metropolitan's Creedon Criticizes Banks as Insurers," *Best's Insurance Management Reports*, Life/Health, May 29, 1984.

[3] Joanne Lipman, "Metropolitan Life to Acquire Century 21; Price is Put at More Than $200 Million," *The Wall Street Journal*, August 21, 1985, p. 5.

[4] Goldsmith, *op. cit.*

[5] James C. Lawson, "Metropolitan to Sell Insurance in Mo. Banks," The *Journal* of *Commerce*, September 20, 1984, p. 7A.

[6] James C. Lawson, "Life Insurers Forming Links to Sell Products," *The Journal of Commerce*, March 5, 1985.

[7] Alfred G. Haggerty, "Bankers See Deregulation Possibility By Year's End," *National Underwriter*, Life and Health edition, February 11, 1984, pp. 1, 41.

[8] "New England Life To Offer Insurance To First Interstate Bancorp Customers," *Best's Insurance Management Reports*, A.M. Best Company, Life/Health, November 11, 1985.

[9] Stephen Piontek, "Met, Ark. S&L Join Forces To Market Products," *National Underwriter*, Life and Health edition, January 18, 1986, p. 1.

5

YOU CAN BANK ON IT

No matter what the arguments are, and no matter what the companies are doing, the idea of banks selling insurance can be a bit intimidating. You might think that my suggesting agents work with, not against, banks is being a bit self-defeating. This is true especially at a time when so many vendors of financial products are moving on to the other's turf.

None of us relishes more competition these days but the fact of the matter is, the competition is here. It's here whether we like it or not. It's here in the form of Sears, Roebuck and Company, American Express, CitiBank, and all those insurance companies developing "alternative" distribution systems. Does that mean that Sears, Roebuck and Company, American Express, CitiBank and the insurance companies are the enemies? Not exactly. They're the competition, but the true enemy is failure to recognize the competition and the irrational resistance to opportunities the competition creates.

The financial world is changing yearly, weekly, daily—almost hourly. The financial superpowers are recognizing the economic challenges of our times and are responding to them. They hear the consumers demanding easier, more convenient financial services, and they are challenging their competition with a variety of new products and creative delivery systems. The movers and shakers of the financial services industry are active participants, not passive observers, in the changing marketplace. And life insurance agents need to be just as active if they are going to compete and survive. Those agents of change take many different approaches, but they share this: They are challenging the old ways of doing business. They question, rather than assume, who should sell what financial products to whom. They question the rules that say banking and insurance should continue to be rivals. They know that agents, brokers and bankers are moving onto one another's turf.

Our supposedly distinct industries aren't so distinct anymore. The differences are eroding because increasingly, the consumer refuses to recognize life insurance and financial services as separate entities. If the consumer doesn't make the distinction, agents can't afford to, either, or the distinction could lead to extinction.

The strategic forays of the giant financial institutions—both banks and insurance companies—have repercussions for all agents as they strive to maintain a strong, competitive foothold in the financial services market. Agents face a marketing challenge to retain their current client base, add new customers and enhance income—and do it all simultaneously.

For many agents, I believe the answer lies in working with smaller, local financial institutions, refining existing products and services, introducing new ones, and creating "financial convenience centers" to mirror the offerings of the larger competitors. This approach makes sense because today's consumers want variety and value provided conveniently. This is where financial institutions will play a vital role. I said that people will turn to financial convenience centers, but notice, I didn't say one-stop financial supermarkets. This is because I don't believe grocery stores, malls, store fronts or department stores will be the final answer.

In the future, financial products will be sold in a manner most convenient and logical for the consumer. For a very large segment of Americans, this may mean doing business where they have traditionally saved and invested—their local bank or thrift. The sale of insurance and other related financial products in such an environment is a natural. When consumers go into a grocery or department store, their minds are on milk, bread or some new drapes—not insurance or money market funds. For the sale of financial products to be successful in the department store atmosphere, the consumer's thinking will have to be reoriented. Customers are already used to coming into banks thinking about financial matters. They think of banks in terms of saving and investing money. With the consumer now regarding life insurance as just another form of saving and investing, buying the products from banks will be very natural.

Banks can be more effective and efficient distributors of insurance because they have two assets that we in the insurance business lack: credibility and frequent face-to-face contact with an expansive customer base. Whether banks deserve the credibility they have is another question, but the fact is that consumers have a better perception of banks than they do of insurance companies.

Every consumer survey places bankers and thrift executives at the top of the list when it comes to trust and credibility. It may be a bitter pill for us to swallow, but insurance executives and agents are rated near the bottom of the list. Consumers believe that banks do a better job than insurance companies in providing good service, respecting individual privacy, treating customers as individuals and giving them their money's worth.

A 1984 survey conducted by the insurance industry asked the public to compare banks and insurance companies as to the knowledge of their employees. Bank personnel were rated more knowledgeable by a margin of 49 percent to 29 percent. Asked to rate the speed and efficiency of service, banks got the nod again, this time by a margin of 67 to 14 percent.[1]

This feeling of trust and confidence that the consumer places in banks means they will be more receptive to products and services bankers offer or endorse. The additional strength offered by banks is the fact that they have access, on a continuing and favorable basis, to a very large base of consumers. It's known, for example, that the average customer walks into a bank office 38 times a year. That's about ten times as much contact as the average consumer has with insurance companies. What a prospecting bonanza!

Those of us marketing insurance know that timing plays a very important part in the buying decision. We look for people who have just been married, had a child, or purchased a new home. Why? We know a "need" has been created, and the prospect is thinking about that new responsibility. It's an old story in homeowners' insurance that a lot of new or increased limit policies are sold when a neighborhood home has burned. The need for adequate insurance has been brought home. When I was an agent, an associate of mine had a gruesome, but successful way of prospecting. He would study the obituary column looking for people who had died young. Thankfully, he did not follow up with the family, but with the neighbors of the person who had died. He felt that the idea of mortality had been brought home to his new prospects. And, you know what, he sold a lot of insurance that way.

These situations highlight the timing aspect of the sale. The problem for most of us selling insurance is that we usually have only one shot at the prospect. If the timing is not right, or the sale is missed, there is usually no chance to go back and make the sale later.

The timing aspect of prospecting and the sale is where banks can play such a useful and productive role. Imagine that each year you have the opportunity to see a prospect 38 times. Even more than that, imagine having the prospect come to see you. Any agent who can't eventually make a sale under those conditions, either is not trying very hard, or must have the personality of an actuary.

When I was starting out as an agent, my trainer would constantly tell me the best way to assure success and build a clientele was to develop "nests" or "centers of influence" which would provide me with a continual base of new prospects. If developed properly, agents can turn banks into the world's largest, and most profitable centers of influence.

All of this paints a rosy picture for banks entering the insurance business, and you may be wondering why they would even bother to deal with agents. Maybe, as some warn, they'll just take all the action for themselves. Bankers can be just as greedy as anyone else. Just like some insurance companies trying to eliminate the agent, some bankers will start with the idea that they can sell insurance without the agent. Just like the insurance companies, though, banks that take this approach will fail and end up coming back to the agent for help.

Believe me when I say that I wouldn't be waxing so eloquent about banks selling insurance if I really thought we weren't walking a two-way street. Agents can be just as helpful to banks as banks can be to agents. While people may feel comfortable buying insurance at a bank, it doesn't necessarily follow that they feel comfortable buying it from a banker. And, as we've already discussed, there are not many bankers who would feel comfortable selling insurance. In fact, the survey that showed such confidence in banks also showed that a whopping 72 percent of those questioned felt the assistance of a professional agent was necessary in purchasing life insurance.[2]

Selling life insurance is not at all like selling bank accounts. The operative word is selling and that word gets little, if any, use in the banker's vocabulary. Quite clearly, life insurance must be sold and that requires the unique marketing expertise and product knowledge that only a life insurance agent possesses. For all the problems of the life insurance industry, even the harshest critics have to concede that agents have the marketing savvy few others can match. Insurance may become a new profit center for banks, but only if it also becomes a new profit center for agents.

The Final Result

As we've seen, bankers face serious problems from narrower profit margins due to increased competition and higher costs. Deregulation has created a need to pay depositors much higher rates, while the cost of maintaining retail branches continues to climb. Banks are looking for ways to make the brick and mortar branch system more profitable. The medium size and regional banks also must find a way to meet the challenges of an emerging national banking system.

In his latest book on banking entitled *The Money Bazaars,* Martin Mayer has a section called, "The Twilight of the Banks." Now, that doesn't sound too encouraging. Mayer's prediction is that banks will command an ever-dwindling share of the financial services market unless they increase what he calls their, "sensitivity to the needs of the users."[3] What he's talking about, of course, is marketing and an expanded product base.

The major problem faced by the life insurance industry is the productivity of the agent. What can we do to put the agents in position to use their unique selling talent more effectively? It's this simple—agents need new customers to sell, and banks need new products to offer. We each have something the other needs. And we have the basis for the perfect marriage, if there is such a thing, because we can make each other stronger by forming new alliances.

Combining banking assets and agent capabilities can form a strong and mutually beneficial partnership. The extensive branch systems and "captive" audiences give agents the chance to reach thousands of potential policyholders directly and efficiently. The benefits for banks are equally noteworthy. Offering insurance provides a chance to retain the loyalty of current bank customers, and extend appeal to new ones by providing a widely purchased and much needed product.

I'm convinced the sale of life insurance through banks and other financial institutions is a logical and natural marketing opportunity. It fulfills such a basic consumer need that, possibly by the end of this century, financial institutions working with professional agents have the opportunity to become the dominant distributors of such products.

With deregulation fast becoming a fact of life, and the sale of insurance through banks a natural and sensible alternative, I don't think we ought to spend much more time debating whether it should be permitted. Rather, I think we should acknowledge that it will be permitted and start discussing how we can take advantage of the opportunity.

Working With Banks and Other Financial Institutions

One of the first things agents will have to learn to practice when working with banks is patience. Bankers seem universally afflicted with the inability to make a decision. This attitude can be very frustrating for an agent who is action oriented.

About four years ago, the management of ITT Life began addressing the distribution question and how it might affect our company and our agents. After exploring many alternatives (including whether we could survive without the agent) we decided that banks would provide, not a way to eliminate the agent but, a great prospecting source to help improve productivity. Immediately after this decision was made, we discussed the opportunity with our field force and started approaching banks. This action took place just as the insurance/banking debate became public.

I started making speeches before banking associations and our home office marketing staff began calling on banks. The initial reaction was very consistent; banks were, at best, apathetic. The suggestion that banks aggressively start selling insurance was met with as much warmth by the bankers as it was by the insurance industry. It has amused me to be at a meeting one day with bankers who were trying to avoid getting into insurance, and then the next day read one of those dire warnings about banks taking over the insurance business.

When it comes to marketing, bankers always take the easy road, and the easy road is not the way to sell insurance. Due to this attitude, bankers initially opted for the list broker approach to selling insurance. With this approach, all banks have to do is make their customer list available to an insurance company or marketing organization. In return, banks receive a fee—usually $100 per 1,000 names—and additional income from "premium collection fees." The insurance company then mass markets products such as accidental death, hospital indemnity, and cancer insurance—great consumer oriented products! The mass marketed sale of "real insurance" was attempted by some banks and insurance companies but generally failed.

In an effort to research the market and attract the interests of banks, ITT Life experimented with the list broker approach but soon discarded it as very inefficient. ITT Life's initial approaches to banks failed because we suggested that "list brokering" was not efficient use of the banks credibility, and suggested they make a firm commitment to the marketing of insurance. As we said to the bankers, "If you start to take Vienna. . . Take Vienna." However, they were not ready for that approach and success eluded us. Even when banks expressed a strong interest in insurance, it took months and months before a decision could be made. Once the decision was made, most banks still wanted to sell insurance by using bank marketing philosophies. (And they wondered why the program was not successful.)

In the course of the last few years, we talked with literally hundreds of banks. Very few, if any, prospects turned into marketing programs mainly because most banks could not make a decision; when they did, it was only a halfhearted commitment. Frankly, the only reason we at ITT Life have hung in there with banks is because we still feel the long-term reward is worth the effort. Despite what many in the life insurance industry fear, banks do not recognize the marketing potential they have. Even if they did, I'm convinced most would not know what to do about it.

However, the situation does seem to be changing. The responses I get at bank meetings are now much more intelligent, and bankers have come to realize that direct mail is not the best way to be successful in insurance. They're still not ready to take the AIB test, but progress is being made. Agents must realize that any negotiations with banks will be long, drawn out and frustrating. Be patient!

Developing Bank Marketing Programs

The bulk of this discussion will center around banks, but agents should not forget the 7,000 thrifts and 22,000 credit unions doing business with millions of potential prospects. Most of these "other" financial institutions are much more aggressive and market oriented than banks. The bank marketing programs we discuss will work just as well, if not better, with these other financial institutions. In addition, there are fewer regulatory issues to be concerned with when dealing with thrifts and credit unions.

One word of caution. When working with banks, be careful not to mention that you may also be working with thrifts. Bankers look down their noses at thrift executives the way medical doctors look down their noses at dentists. I've heard many bankers refer to thrift executives as "failed bankers." It's an interesting position for bankers to take, especially when considered from a marketing standpoint, where most bankers can't carry a thrift executive's passbook. Whatever, stand warned about the banker's sensitive feelings. (If you tell a banker what I just said, I'll deny it.)

Marketing Consultant

Banks and life insurance companies like to hire "consultants" to help them make decisions. This happens because people working in corporations, especially bureaucratic organizations like insurance companies and banks, quickly come to value job security above all else. Ever wonder why home office executives are always in "committee meetings"? They soon learn that a "committee" can't be fired. No one has to take responsibility for decisions reached by a committee.

Consultants perform the same service for the bureaucrat. Consultants are set up as experts. It is not unusual for a consultant to reach the same conclusions as the person who hired him. If the right decision is made, those who retained the consultant can claim credit. If the programs don't work, it's the consultant's fault and his contract is not renewed. The consultant game is a nice one because it creates work for a number of people and provides good protection for the bureaucrat. Bankers are among the world's best bureaucrats.

Agents can take advantage of this situation by offering their experience in insurance to the bank. To do this, you will have to be independent and offer a good service. You simply cannot use the idea of being a consultant as a way to get your company's products into the bank.

As a consultant, you can perform a very valuable service for the bank. The first step is to get to know the management of the bank and the objectives they are seeking. After that task has been accomplished, you must do your research and develop a comprehensive marketing plan for the bank. You may find, initially, that banks are more concerned with not upsetting any checking account holders (even though they are losing money on the accounts) than they are in making money selling insurance. Under these conditions, statement stuffers offering insurance service may be the best way to start. You may realize that this approach is not the best, but it would be a start and could keep you involved while you convince the bank to explore other programs.

As a consultant, you are going to have to be independent from insurance companies. You have to be in a position to look for the best policies and contracts available. As a bank marketing consultant, you will be in the position to recommend whether the bank acquires an agency, starts one from scratch, or forms a joint venture with an insurance company or existing agency.

The great part about this consulting arrangement is that the bank will pay you for your expertise. The fee would depend upon your negotiating ability, but I would suggest a flat fee of, say, $25,000 to $50,000 with a percentage of future income to the bank. I know of one situation where a bank paid an independent "insurance consultant" $4,000 per week for a guaranteed six-month period.

The consulting fee should really be the easiest part. One of the best things about the fee arrangement is it gives you an indication of the bank's seriousness about insurance. Insurance companies may have the money to wait for recalcitrant banks to make decisions, but most agents can't. If the bank is not willing to pay for your service, they are not very interested in distributing insurance. The objective is to get the bank hooked, but not to give your experience away.

The most important part of any deal should be the percentage factor. Bankers do not recognize just how much money they can make from the distribution of insurance, so they are very willing to give away a piece of something that does not seem significant. I would encourage agents making consulting arrangements with banks to shoot for five to ten percent of the gross bank insurance income over a five to ten-year period. Once the insurance program is set up, you can either move on to the next one, or structure the operation so you have a continuing key role.

There are many advantages to the consulting approach, but the big one is that you are the one in control. Rather than depending on what insurance or banking companies will do to, or for, you this approach puts you in the position of doing something for the insurance companies. You'd be surprised how they treat you when you have all the power and control.

Of course, it's not logical to assume agents are able to go out and make consulting deals with the big banks, but that doesn't have to be done. Agents will find their best opportunities working with some of the 15,000 small or local operations. These banks need the profits from the sale of insurance just as much as agents need a better way to sell. Working together will benefit both you and the bank. Try the consulting approach to banks; you may be surprised just how effective it can be.

Renting Space in a Bank Lobby

Renting space in a bank lobby has become the "in" thing to do when it comes to marketing insurance. This arrangement developed as an attempt to circumvent the regulations that prevent banks from soliciting insurance or receiving direct commissions.

The Comptroller of the Currency has ruled that federal banks may "lease" space in their lobby to an insurance operation so long as the bank is not directly selling insurance. (It should be noted that various state laws may supersede the Comptroller's ruling.) The key point of the ruling is that the rent can be pegged as a percentage of the sales made in the lobby. I know dealing with the government can be a little confusing but, in the old days, getting a percentage of the premium sold was called receiving commissions.

A number of big banks and insurance companies have jumped at the chance to take advantage of this ruling. The best examples are Bank of America teaming up with Capital Holding Corporation; First Interstate in a joint venture with Safeco; Metropolitan working with banks in Missouri; and the famous Craddock experiment with Aetna Insurance and a bank in Tennessee.

Under the lease arrangement, the insurance company or local agency provides the products and the people to sell the insurance. The bank just clears out a corner of the lobby and says, "Go to it." From the bank's point of view, this option offers the advantage of being able to enter the insurance business with very little effort and financial risk. One day the bank offers no insurance and the next day it has a full-fledged operation. The leasing arrangement has been attractive to banks because it appeals to their passive marketing philosophy. They can offer insurance in their lobby, just like those little pamphlets in the rack, without getting involved.

On the one hand, these are promising arrangements because they create the opportunity to "get in the door." Under present restrictions of noninvolvement, however, I have some questions as to whether they will be successful. The participating bank must go to great pains to avoid any hint of involvement in the sale. Actual barriers are set up in the lobby to make sure the insurance operation is identified as a separate entity. As it's structured today, the lease approach to selling insurance in banks may be doomed for failure and could damage the whole idea of banks selling insurance.

Let me explain myself. I've had the opportunity to visit a couple of the "rental" offices opened by Bank of America. It's very sad. I call them the Hare-Krishna offices. You see these little insurance people actually shuttled off behind some potted plants in a corner of the lobby. It reminds me of the little boxes they put the Hare-Krishna people in at the airports so they won't bother people. Travelers can go up to the Hare-Krishna people if they want and the airport can claim they have not suppressed freedom of speech. If you notice, more and more of the boxes at the airports are empty because the people with the message can't get to the people they want to sell. For the same reason, we may see many of these "rental lobby" arrangements fail. If that happens, those in both banking and insurance who have been against the idea of banks selling insurance will say, "See, I told you it was a bad idea."

There are two reasons banks can be successful distributing insurance: credibility with the consumer and; access to a large number of potential customers. The rental idea, as it's structured today, is a bad idea because it gives the bank a false sense of being in the insurance business. Bankers are not using their credibility with the large number of people they can access.

Let's have a little quiz. Are the airlines in the insurance business because Mutual Of Omaha rents booths at the airports? Which situation would sell more insurance: a Mutual of Omaha booth in the lobby of the airport terminal or; having the pilot of the plane go up and down the aisle selling insurance just before takeoff? The pilot would have access to people, and he would have a certain amount of credibility.

It's my belief that insurance sales through banks will not be successful unless the bankers become involved. Just putting some agents in a lobby, and then trying to avoid any contact with them, will not result in successful insurance sales. If bankers don't, or can't, use their credibility with the consumer to recommend insurance services, all the traffic through a lobby will be of no value. If traffic is the only objective, you might just as well go rent space from a gas station.

Insurance sales in banks will not become successful until it becomes an integral part of the entire bank operation. Today, it's natural for the customer services officer to refer business to the loan officer, and he/she, in turn, to the trust officer. When insurance planning can be linked to that cycle, the full sales potential will be realized. Unless the agent recognizes the "foot-in-the-door" benefits of bank leasing arrangements, I would not recommend such programs until full deregulation allows bank involvement in sales.

Joint Venture Arrangements

Ultimately, I believe the joint venture program will prove to be the most successful for the bank and the agent. Under this plan the agent, or more likely an independent agency, enters into a marketing arrangement with a local, independent bank. The bank provides the endorsement and the prospects, and the agency provides the agents to make the actual sales. For example, the bank would provide a list of mortgages made during the last month and the agency would go out and offer a bank sponsored "mortgage redemption plan." An agent could be placed in the bank lobby and identified as the bank's insurance officer. Bank customers could be approached by direct mail or telemarketing, and identified prospects would then be contacted by the agency.

Banks will be compensated by receiving an "override" on all business sold. The increase in production for the agency due to the activity and endorsement of the bank should more than make up for the cost of splitting commissions. This joint venture agency arrangement may not become the most prevalent, but it is a good one and will achieve wide acceptance in the future. The agency gets to maintain its independence and yet has a valuable prospecting source that will allow it to recruit and attract high quality agents. The bank develops a new profit center with new products and services to offer. From the banker's point of view, the bank does not have to get involved in the insurance operation.

Bank Owned Agencies

No doubt when deregulation comes, a large number of banks will acquire or start a captive agency. Many savings and loans have opted for this approach to their insurance marketing. Working for or managing a bank owned agency has some advantages and disadvantages.

The major advantage to be gained from working with a bank owned agency is that you know the bank is fully committed to the insurance program. Agents working with the bank agency will have the resources and credibility of the institution backing up their prospecting and sales. In fact, prospecting is the last thing bank agents will be concerned about.

A disadvantage in working with a bank owned agency is the fact that you may have exchanged one master, the life insurance company, for another—the bank. The insurance company may not be the agent's true friend, but at least most home office executives understand insurance. (I've been told many times that is not true in my case.) Bankers may attempt to manage an agency the same way other bank departments are run, and that would be the worst way to manage an agency.

One of the problems that will be encountered either working directly for a bank as the "insurance officer" or managing the bank's agency is the current bank philosophy of compensation. Bankers may have a great deal of credibility and prestige, but they don't get paid much money. Banks still have the philosophy of pay by pecking order. No one in the bank makes more money than the president. The insurance officer or agency manager could not make more money than the executives to whom they report. This attitude works fine (or at least they think it does) for banks, but it does not work well for commissioned sales people. I consider it a sign of success to have scores of ITT Life agents making more money than I, but any self-respecting bank president would never allow this to happen. Unless such attitudes change, the bank owned agency may not be able to attract the best agents or management.

Developing Marketing Programs

When an agent begins negotiating with banks, it's important to structure initial marketing programs to fit the mind-set of the banker. Remember that bankers are still interested in two things—increased deposits and more customers. If insurance programs can be structured in such a way as to enhance these objectives they stand a better chance of gaining the bank's support.

A good example of this approach would be an Individual Retirement Account (IRA) cross-sell insurance marketing program. Banks view IRAs as bank products so any program that would enhance IRA sales would find bank acceptance. Under this option, bank IRA customers could be shown how to buy life insurance with tax-deferred dollars. IRA packages could be designed to include a "self-completion feature" in the event of the participant's death or disability. The bank sees itself benefiting from additional customer IRA deposits as well as from the insurance income.

The key in developing or presenting bank marketing programs is to tie sales efforts to the strength of the institution. If the bank makes a number of mortgages, suggest a good mortgage life and disability protection plan. If the bank specializes in small business customers, a good business overhead protection plan or franchise group would fit well. In short, take advantage of the bank market and put the emphasis in the areas where the bank works and feels comfortable.

Golden Rules

Now that I've explained why you should consider working with, not against, banks in the sale of insurance and have offered some approaches to use, I'd like to share with you a few rules that I think will be essential for successful joint ventures.

Rule One: Make sure the bank is fully committed to the insurance program. Unless you know for sure that senior management is supporting the venture, don't waste your time. Without full management support, the very best marketing plan will fail.

Rule Two: Keep the program simple. We in the insurance industry have tended to make the purchase of life insurance a very confusing encounter for the consumer. Don't repeat this mistake with bank customers. I don't believe we need to offer many different policies from many different companies. Pick the best program available and go with it. One of the advantages of working with banks is consumer confidence. If you have a good, simple and competitive plan, it will work.

Rule Three: Don't let the banks take the "discount brokerage" approach to insurance. As we pointed out earlier, banks still view themselves as a "service" organization. They have a tendency to take a lot of products, put them out on the counter and then wait for the consumer to make a selection. As we know, that will not work with insurance. A smorgasbord of policies and programs creates too many options and stymies consumer action. If a bank will not allow you to recommend and sell, walk away.

Rule Four: I've said it before, but it's worth saying again—be patient. Banks are not marketing organizations. Banks do not understand marketing; they offer a service and wait for the phone to ring. The opportunity is worth the wait, but it will call for patience.

I suppose all this talk about bank marketing programs and various joint venture options may seem a bit challenging. Yet, there is a great amount of excitement and opportunity within that challenge. If banks and independent insurance agents can bring together their separate but powerful strengths, the future will belong to them. Suddenly, banks will become more than banks or thrifts, they'll become known as wide-angle financial institutions. They'll have new and more satisfied customers, increased deposits and new profit centers. The agent can view the future with a much brighter outlook. Banks have the resources which, when properly used, will help the agents spend their time doing what they do best—selling—not prospecting or servicing.

However, it's up to the agents to take the lead. Let the traditionalists, the laggards in our industry continue to fight this opportunity. Agents should be the ones to bring fresh ideas and talent to the changing financial services scene. Agents must accept all the risks that bank involvement presents, but if they do, they will also enjoy all the profits that will go with success.

Chapter V Notes

[1] "Marketing of Life Insurance by Banks," Social Research Services, American Council of Life Insurance, March 1985, p. 26.

[2] Ibid, p. 53.

[3] Martin Mayer, *The Money Bazaars,* (Dutton, New York) 1984, first edition.

6

DISTRIBUTION 1990

"Sell yourself, your service, your consulting capability, and the availability of a broad range of reliable products. Stay away from specific brands unless they're heavily identified with your kind of image."[1] These words were written by Charles W. Brodhead, president and co-founder of The Communications Support Group. In very concise fashion, I believe Mr. Brodhead has suggested a formula for agent survival and success.

The agents who emerge as winners in the distribution revolution will sell their service and consulting capability to the consumer. That's nothing new, agents have been doing that for generations, but the future will see a shift in this emphasis. In the past, agents tended to identify themselves with one company. With all companies selling basically the same products—whole life and term—identification with one specific company was not a problem. However, due to the variety of products that will be available in the future, and the fact that Universal life from one company may not be the same or as competitive as that offered by another company, identification with one company could be a problem.

The future agents will have to establish their independence and prove, especially to the sophisticated consumer, that they can offer the best products for a particular need. Mr. Brodhead confirms this point by suggesting agents be careful not to be identified with a "specific brand" of product. Agents who learn this secret will be the big winners. As a result, we will see a basic change in the structure of the distribution systems—especially the classic career system.

Classic Distribution Systems

For most of this century, the life insurance industry has used three basic distribution systems: 1) the career agency; 2) Personal Producing General Agents (PPGAs) and; 3) brokerage. The career agency system deserves much of the credit for the development of the life insurance industry and its agents. Without the career agency, the industry would not be as large as it is today, and millions of individuals would not have been able to enjoy the fruits of a life insurance career.

The classic career agency has been based on the concept of captive agents representing a sponsoring company, virtually on an exclusive basis. The career agency is usually directed by an "independent" general agent who recruits individuals who have never sold life insurance. The general agent instructs the new agents as to the structure of product, teaches them how to prospect, and drills them on ways to make the sale. While all this is happening, the new agents are being supported financially. The parent company and the agency combined will invest nearly $200,000 to recruit and train one successful agent. In the past, a successful agent has been defined as one who produces an average of one application per week or, if the agent is really good, makes about $35,000 per year to qualify for the Million Dollar Round Table.

With few exceptions, these agencies are brick and mortar offices usually in the high-rent district of town. They are carpeted, wallpapered, and equipped with the latest in office automation. They employ clerks and secretaries to help service agents, process business and correspondence. Someone must always be on hand to answer the telephone and meet with policyholders seeking service. Larger agencies usually have a training or advanced underwriting specialist, and many have unit managers. In short, career agencies, as they're structured today, are an expensive operation.

The PPGA system is a fraternity of those who have graduated from a career agency. Those operating as PPGAs were generally successful as career agents but felt confined by the controls necessary to maintain a career agency. In exchange for leaving the comfortable "nest" of the career agencies, the PPGAs receive increased compensation, the opportunity to make the business truly their own, and most importantly, the psychic benefits of independence.

The brokerage distribution system developed, not really as an independent system, but as a supplement to both the career agency and PPGAs. There have been very few "true brokers" in the life insurance industry. The need to find a solution for the special problem, the substandard risk, the low cost term policy, or the supplemental health plan provided an opportunity that brokerage companies have successfully filled. Brokerage companies piggybacked on the training and investment of career agencies but, in return, offered products and services that could not be economically provided by the career company.

Despite substantial differences in structure, financing, and method of operation, these distribution systems have had one thing in common—the agent. Today, the distribution systems are under attack and will undergo some major changes in the future. In response to these pressures there are some who will try to develop agent-less systems. However, that strategy won't work. In spite of the changes we face, one thing will remain constant—the industry's dependence on the agent to make the actual sale. The life insurance industry will not operate without agents, but how the agents operate in the industry will change.

In order to protect themselves against those trying to eliminate the agent and to assure their place in the future, agents must recognize the revolutionary changes taking place in the distribution systems. Actually, agents must do more than simply recognize change. To recognize change is one thing; to participate in change and its direction is, by far, the most important act for agents. Agents must decide which of the new or evolving systems will be best for them and help make that system become a successful reality. If agents don't take action, someone will do it for them, and they may not like the results.

The Future of the Career Agency

There are many who don't want to admit it, but the classic career agency system is dying. It may already be dead. Sure, there will be aberrations but, except for those few who establish a certain market niche, the classic career agency's impact on the life insurance industry will be drastically reduced, if not eliminated.

As I said, there are those who will deny the career agency is dying and will call my comments anti-agent. With close inspection, however, you'll find those to be the same ones who refused to admit that whole life had seen its best days. They will be the ones who swear allegiance to the career agency while they seek alternative distribution systems. Just as the handwriting was on the whole life policy long before industry leaders recognized it, movement away from the classic career agency is now well underway.

LIMRA issued a report on the outlook for the ordinary insurance distribution system that said, "Between 1974 and 1981, the level of new-blood ordinary agent recruiting declined about 23 percent. In 1981, while the overall recruiting activity was down 7 percent, recruiting of inexperienced agents declined 13 percent. To put these data into context, it should be recognized that 14 of the largest agency-building companies contributed 64 percent of all the ordinary recruits in 1981. This same group of companies accounted for 72 percent of all new blood inducted into the industry in that year, thus carrying the burden of the industry's manpower building. While approximately two of every three agents that are contracted are new to the industry, for this group of companies the figure is four of every five."[2]

The LIMRA report seemed to confirm the demise of the classic career agency when it reported, "The history of the United States insurance distribution system is one of exclusive representation. The pure franchise general agency system has largely given way to the managerial system and a subsidized company general agency system, largely because the high costs involved in agency development were unaffordable by individual independent general agents. Today's economy does not signal a return to the completely independent general agency philosophy as a practical operating option."[3]

You know there's change in the air when classic career agency companies like Prudential run ads claiming they have almost 50,000 brokers under contract. Prudential proudly points out that brokerage business has increased over 250% since 1981. Metropolitan, the other pillar of the career agency, has been doing extensive advertising—looking for brokers.

Some companies have come to view their captive agencies as something more than just a distribution system for company products. For them, the distribution system is considered an asset just like any other investment owned by the company. The current system is not providing adequate return so, in response, the company puts the agents out for "hire" to another company.

In 1984, Prudential announced it was leaving the individual disability income field and "selling" its agents to Paul Revere. With this action, Prudential was admitting it could not be totally successful in the health business, and its agents could not be productive enough selling only life insurance. Paul Revere, selling primarily through exclusive agents, admitted it needed a broader distribution system for its products. By "selling" the agency system to Paul Revere, Prudential is assuming the role of a super general agent and is attempting to recoup, via override, some of its heavy investment in the career agent. I make this point, not to be critical, but to emphasize changes evolving in the classic agency system.

We will be seeing more and more of these arrangements and agents should recognize they are, in effect, being treated as a chattel. If the deal made for the agent by the company is helpful, that's fine. In contrast, maybe the agent should be the one selling his services, not a company that looks upon the agent as an asset that can be traded around at whim.

North American Life joined a long list of companies when it announced in 1983 the complete elimination of its career agency system. Richard Hanson, vice president for individual marketing, discussing North American's move away from the career agency, suggested the best way for his company to sell its products in the future was to convert its distribution system from a branch operation to one based on independent general agents.[4] In 1985, Penn Mutual, with little or no warning, closed or consolidated a large number of career agencies.

Jim Anderson, of the actuarial and consulting firm Tillinghast, Nelson & Warren, Inc., wrote in July of 1983, "A growing crisis exists in the traditional distribution system of the life insurance industry. Temporarily, the crisis has been masked by increased commission earnings associated with increased replacement activity, but this phenomenon will soon have spent its force." Mr. Anderson further pointed out, ". . . the cost of maintaining existing distribution systems is well beyond the level required to be economic."[5]

As suggested previously, the biggest problem facing the classic career agency system is that products being sold today and forecast for the future do not have the profit margins needed to support the cost of recruiting, training and financing neophyte agents. Many companies that recognize this problem are trying to save the career agency by doing two things: 1) moving the agents into higher and higher income markets and; 2) attempting to offer a wide variety of products identified by the general concept of financial services.

There is the assumption that by working with higher income prospects larger cases will be sold and productivity will increase vertically. The agent may not be able to increase the number of sales, but larger sales will make up the difference. By offering a variety of financial service products the companies are attempting to improve productivity and income along a horizontal plane. Make a little on each product, but sell a lot of them, seems to be the objective.

I don't believe either of these measures will allow the traditional career agency to remain as the dominant distributor of insurance products. Just how many high income people are there? Less than five percent of the population makes in excess of $60,000. How many agents can make a living selling insurance to five percent of the population? Walter H. Zultowski, LIMRA's second vice president of Industry Research, has pointed out that after the 5.8 million affluent households are divided among the current number of agents, the outcome would be only 24 clients each. Further, a survey conducted by Research and Forecasts, a subsidiary of Ruder Finn & Rotman, and reported in the *National Underwriter,* concluded ". . . the degree of trust in the insurance agent as a financial adviser goes down as the respondent's income goes up."[6]

The idea of offering a wide variety of products to achieve the degree of success needed to support the career agency will not work, either. The reaction of the consumer to this approach is critical and, we may find, not very receptive. A recent experience I had is not very scientific, but it could be very telling. An acquaintance mentioned that he called his friend and agent who worked with a traditional career agency company. The receptionist who answered the phone identified the office as a "financial services company." This individual knew it was an insurance office, but didn't care, because he wanted some information about his policy. When he chided the agent about the "financial services" the response was very defensive. "Don't you know," said the agent, "we're the fourth largest financial services company in America!" The caller really wasn't bothered by the response of his agent, but he did say to me, "Why are you insurance guys always trying to hide what you do? You can say financial services all you want, but I know the best thing you do is sell insurance, so why not admit it?"

If the companies want to change their career agencies and agents into stockbrokers or financial planners, that's fine. However, using a wide variety of financial products as a mask for the sale of insurance in order to save the career agency system will fail. In fact, success for the strategy of multiple products sold by a captive salesperson, under any conditions, may itself be questionable. *BusinessWeek* understood this when it ran a cover story entitled, "Merrill Lynch's Big Dilemma—Its strong broker system is a costly handicap in a deregulated world." The article pointed out, "The company's greatest strength—its retail system of 431 branch offices and 8,763 brokers—has also become its greatest handicap. By funneling nearly all of its growing number of offerings through its brokers, Merrill generates huge sales volume. But because its brokers get a cut of all they sell, this approach is very expensive. And its inflexibility makes Merrill vulnerable at a time when discount brokering and other low-cost distribution methods are gaining market share."[7] Merrill Lynch faces these problems despite the fact that each one of their brokers has over 100 different financial products, including life insurance, to offer.

The idea of offering multiple products, of selling a little of something to everyone, is a nice idea and might seem a logical solution to the career agency productivity problem. As Merrill Lynch has learned, though, such a strategy also brings multiple costs. Products have to support their existence, and it's not economically viable to believe a firm or agency can offer a number of "loss leaders" just so the main product—life insurance or stocks—can be sold. The cost of offering a wide variety of financial products in the Merrill Lynch system means the average broker must produce gross commissions of at least $250,000 a year, just to justify his existence.

Is there any reason to believe the life insurance career agency, offering a wide variety of products, will be any more successful than Merrill Lynch? Are we nearing a time when the average career agent will have to produce $250,000 in gross commissions just to justify his existence?

Those who offer product multiplicity as a solution to the current agency distribution problems are missing the point. The problem today is not getting more products for agents to sell, it's getting more people for agents to sell. People recognize the need for insurance, although most people do not own enough insurance. Agents are very talented and if they can get in front of enough people, they will sell enough insurance. With the introduction of the new interest sensitive policies the agent will, once again, have competitive products to offer. If the agent can get in front of people in an efficient, logical and convenient manner, the so-called productivity problems will go away. Successful life insurance agents of the future will probably sell fewer, not more, product styles.

A study of various leading agencies will show a strong emphasis on pension sales and payroll deduction plans. Why have 401(K) plans been such a rage of late? (They have also created rage at the IRS offices.) Programs like 401(K), and before that Retired Lives Reserves (RLR) are easier sales because of their tax advantages. In addition, I believe there is another factor which is the agent being able to make multiple sales simultaneously. The agent working for agencies specializing in these markets is able to increase productivity because he or she sees more people on a favorable basis. The tax advantages help, but it is not the critical issue. Most of today's growing agencies have some kind of market sponsorship or endorsement such as working with a union, employer or (heaven forbid) a bank. As we move into the future, distribution organizations that can provide multiple markets for the agent to work, rather than multiple products for the agent to sell, will be the most successful.

A further weakness in offering multiple products as the solution to agency problems is human nature. As humans, we tend to get comfortable with one pattern and then stick to it. Rarely will salespeople become a jack-of-all-trades when it comes to products and markets. As LIMRA has discovered, ". . . research evidence supports the observation that the absolute number of sales made by an agent plateaus after a few years of experience. This observation of plateauing in number of sales is probably one of the most critical in understanding the dynamics of products and distribution strategies, ergo, the future of the agency system.

It stands to reason that if the number of sales that an agent makes is relatively inflexible or fixed, in the short run, a new product will be sold only at the expense of some other product already being sold."[8]

Part of Merrill Lynch's problems in offering more than 100 different products is that they found their better producers prefer to have a variety of products available, but tend to sell only a few of them. The broker may specialize in bonds or the futures market but completely ignore new issues and tax exempts. The brokers get comfortable with a certain set of products and stick with them.

It's an age-old feeling among life insurance people that property and casualty agents could sell a great deal of life insurance—if they would only try. But we all know the casualty agent who sells life is a rare person. One large casualty company recently had a major marketing strategy aimed at its agents. The company felt success could be reached if it could get the casualty agents to produce one life application . . . per year. The casualty agents do not sell life insurance because they are not comfortable with the product. Even the most successful direct writing casualty companies, like Allstate and State Farm, have found that only 25 percent of their agents' income is from life insurance sales. Look inside a career agency and you will see individuals working and staying in fairly well-defined markets. Those who specialize in estate planning rarely sell pension products. The agent working in the business insurance market rarely sells a family rider.

The classic career agency will not be a major factor in the future, but the career agent will. We will not see an end to the career agent, but we will see a new definition of career agent, and that person will operate out of a new structure. The new distribution structure will not only enable the agent to survive, it will stimulate agent growth, productivity, and income. The career agent of the future will be much more in control of his future and be in a much better position to offer competitive products and services.

Career Agencies of the Future

The career agencies of the future will be divided into two different types of operations: the independent field marketing organization (FMO) and; the sponsored agency. The independent field marketing organization will become the dominant distributor of insurance products for the life insurance industry. The sponsored agency will be involved in joint venture arrangements and be owned by a financial institution, or be associated with an organization that has access to large numbers of prospects.

The Field Marketing Organization

A field marketing organization might best be defined as a group of independent, professional, highly qualified individuals who have banded together to produce large volumes of premium, usually from a specific and well-defined market.

The individuals who form FMOs will be highly motivated and have a strong sense of entrepreneurial spirit. They will have extensive, successful experience in a specific market such as salary savings, pensions, estate planning or basic needs selling. Their reputation, abilities and established market will allow them to attract similar producers and pass on their knowledge to newer agents.

In 1986 terms, the minimum size FMO would have annual production of at least $1 million in paid premiums. However, it will not be unusual to see marketing organizations producing tens of millions of dollars in premiums. The strength of the marketing organization will be its ability to independently control large amounts of premium. We all know that companies respond warmly to large amounts of premium. As a result, the producer will be, for the first time, on an equal footing with the companies.

Certainly there have been career agencies that have produced large amounts of volume but, many will agree, they are fairly rare and, for the most part, they are under control of the company, not the agent. In the past I've seen clear evidence that, for the sake of control, companies would rather have five agencies producing $400,000 in premium than one producing $2 million.

The relationship between the company and the FMO will be viewed more as a joint venture arrangement between a manufacturer and distributor. With the power of production the FMO will be able to sit down with the companies to design product, compensation structure, representatives' contracts and sales support materials. FMOs will not be tied to a company by exclusive contracts, but will tend, because of established relationships, to work with relatively few companies. One or two companies may be designated to provide life products, while another may issue needed disability policies, and still another might offer annuities.

When discussion of changing distribution systems gets serious, many raise the question: Who will recruit, finance and train the new agent? That's a very valid question, but I think it is focused incorrectly. We should be more concerned about the future of the new agent if we don't change the current system! As we've already seen, it's getting more expensive and difficult for the classic career agency to perform the recruiting role. As we'll see later, the current direction of the career agency will exacerbate the problem more than solve it. As part of the changing relationship, the FMO will assume the recruiting, training, selection, supervision and motivation of the respective FMO members. Because the FMOs will be run by very experienced field people and will operate in a specific, well-defined market, it will be able to get the new agent into production very quickly. The FMO's structure and financing system will allow it to be the primary recruiting system of the future.

It's important to understand that because the FMO will be financing the building of the agent base, the contractual relationship between the agent and the company will change. Under the traditional career agency system, because it was financially supporting the recruiting and training of the new agent, the company both contracted and controlled the agent. In the future, as part of an FMO, the agent will be "appointed" to sell for the company but the long-term relationship is with the FMO, not the company.

Compensation and the FMO

Basic compensation paid to the FMO will be on a "grossed-up" basis. By that I mean the FMO will negotiate with the company as to the amount of commissions priced into the product, and the entire amount will be paid directly to the FMO. Expenses that would otherwise have to be retained by the company to pay for the marketing, recruiting, training and a variety of other services, will now be available to the FMO. The FMO will work with the company to balance compensation with product value because it will recognize that the higher the commissions, the less competitive the product. Once the commissions are determined, the entire amount will be passed along to the FMO. It is the FMO, not the company, who will determine how the commissions are split among the producers.

The concept of paying each agency the same percentage commission regardless of size, as in the career agency system, will vanish as successful FMOs emerge. Companies will be competing for the business produced by the FMOs and, as a result, they will be willing to develop compensation systems that provide increased income based upon the size and quality of business produced by the FMO. Since companies will no longer control the production unit, they will want to tie FMO compensation directly to the profitability of the business produced. In fact, the very large organizations will be able to participate in the actual profitability of the business sold through what are coming to be called "agent owned life companies."

Under this arrangement, a separate reinsurance company is established by the insurance company and the FMO. Both the insurance company and the FMO, usually including the producers, become the stockholders of the new company. After certain minimums are met, a portion of the business produced by the FMO is assigned to this company. The agent develops the business that is assigned to the agent owned company and the main company provides all the accounting and administration. As the profits emerge, the value of the reinsurance company increases as does the equity value of the participants. Such a program allows the FMO and its members to participate directly in the profits of the business they sell.

As a result, one of the most discussed subjects in the life insurance industry today is the concept of an agent owned insurance company (AOC). The concept is a good one. The agent not only receives commissions for selling business, but also has the opportunity to participate in the future profits (if any) of that same block of business. What could be better?

We also must recognize and acknowledge that the concept has great appeal to the ego—something rarely lacking from the makeup of a successful producer. It's much more fun to be a capitalist than a captive. Admittedly, the idea of an AOC does have sex appeal but, with closer examination, it may be missing the romance of true love. I believe that on balance agents will find that it is not to their advantage to become involved with AOC's. The concept of an AOC sounds great—owning stock, sharing in the profits, getting rich. However, remember the old adage—if it looks too good to be true, it probably is!

As the president of a life insurance company, believe it or not, I am all in favor of AOC's. I'm very happy when someone in the field comes to me and says they want to start or get involved in a reinsurance deal. I know that as a result of such an arrangement ITT Life will benefit in the following ways: 1) we'll probably get most of the agent's business; 2) because the agent is involved financially, the business we receive will be of high quality; 3) with the agent making an investment in the business, our cost and risk is reduced and; 4) the company will have a long-term relationship with the agent because the agent will have to wait for the profits to emerge. As long as the AOC is real and not a sham, I'll take all the deals I can get. The AOC can also benefit agents but I suggest they be wary. Many of the deals I've seen proposed or in action are in reality sham reinsurance arrangements.

One must remember that a company will not enter into an AOC arrangement out of the goodness of its heart or in an effort to help the agent. Far from it. There is nothing wrong with the companies benefiting from the arrangement—it has to be good for both sides. Yet, I'm not sure agents have as much to gain from the arrangement.

When I say most programs are a sham, I don't mean the companies are trying to cheat the agents. Because agents usually can't afford to put up the necessary capital, companies have created what could be referred to as "window dressing arrangements." These may look like reinsurance arrangements but, at best, they are nothing more than a fancy bonus arrangement for good production. What many agents may not realize is that owning and operating a life insurance company is a very expensive and long-term venture.

Owning a life insurance company means having to deal with agents who always want better products, higher commissions and less underwriting. Growing life insurance companies are cash-eaters, not cash-cows.

When everything is added—commissions, underwriting and marketing expenses, taxes and reserves—the average life insurance company is going to invest anywhere from $20 to $50 of surplus for every $100 of first-year premium received by the company. For example, if an agent sells a policy with a $1,000 annual premium, the company will spend, on average, $400 of its surplus (plus the $1,000 premium) just to get the policy in force. Profits on that policy are pegged as a percentage of the invested surplus. (Most companies aim for 12 percent to 17 percent.) When you consider that a policy must usually be in force at least four years before the company fully recovers the surplus, and ten years of premium must be paid before full profits are recovered, it becomes apparent that investing in new life insurance policies may indeed be exciting, but it is not the surest investment in the world. And you can see why as a company president, I'm more than happy to have agents volunteer to share the risk.

Agents should recognize that under the classic compensation arrangement, most of their profits (commissions) are fronted, while company profits emerge on the back-end. The AOC arrangement gives the agents a chance to make a little more money (but not much if you consider the time value of money and the risk element) but defers a good deal of income over a minimum of ten years. And there is the chance the agent will never get the money that was earned! We've heard stories about "leveling" commissions. Most agents have resisted such an approach but seem willing to jump headlong into reinsurance deals that not only level income but stir in the added ingredient that the income may never be paid.

The only way companies are going to share a portion of the profits associated with a group of policies is if the agent is willing to make an investment—by actually putting up cash or reducing commissions—in the business. Anyone who believes the companies are going to make the full investment required to put new business in force, and then be willing to give up as much as 50 percent of the future profits, is standing on the Brooklyn Bridge gazing at his swampland. Agents should recognize that if they are not asked to make an initial and continuing investment in AOC, they are not in a real AOC.

As I said, the idea of agents sharing in the profits of business they produce is a good one. If I owned a life insurance company, one of the first things I would do is set it up so agents could become fully involved. I'd like to see them become actual stockholders of the company and be concerned about the company's future.

I think it's also important for agents to be able to participate, beyond pure commissions, in the benefits of high quality business. I'd also like to suggest that from an agent's standpoint, there are better ways than an AOC to accomplish this objective.

For example, ITT Life has established a profitability index and productivity bonus. Under these programs the agent, because he puts up no portion of the investment, does not share in the return on that investment. However, the agent does get a healthy share of any increase over our expected return. Let's say we are selling a product that assumes Linton B, or nearly 80 percent persistency. If the assumed conditions are met, the company will receive its 15 percent return on the invested surplus and the agent will have earned the commission. All should be fair. However, if the agent sells business that, let's say, has Linton A persistency, then profits would be better than expected. Since the agent was responsible, he or she should be able to share in this increase.

Under the plan in use at ITT Life, the agent receives 60 percent of any such increase in profits from the business. Likewise, if an agent produces business that generates less than anticipated profits, the agent is asked to share 60 percent of the loss in the form of charged back commissions. The advantage for the agent under this plan is he or she receives the normal commissions and has the opportunity to receive increased income if the business is better than anticipated. Additionally, the agent's increased income is fronted to him in the first or second year of the policy; the company still must wait ten years for the full excess profits to emerge. The only thing missing from this scenario is the ego gratification that comes from owning some stock in a life insurance company.

One other way ITT Life has sought to involve the agent in the profitability of the business without forcing him or her to make an investment is by paying increased income for increased productivity. The fact of the matter is that it's less costly for a company to support an agency doing $3 million of premium than it is for one doing $500,000. The larger agency is usually better organized, more independent and less in need of specific support. Because products are not priced with this idea in mind (i.e. each agency sells the same policy with no difference in premium or commissions) the result is that larger agencies pay a portion of the cost of supporting smaller operations, or the home office duplicates the support of the larger agency. Under our productivity concept, some of the larger agencies could be paid up to 15 percent higher commissions, as they should be, simply because they are more cost efficient to support.

Combined, these profitability and productivity indexes will probably return more money faster to agents than under any type of AOC arrangement. The AOC arrangement can be a good one, but I would encourage agents exploring such options to make sure they are following the lead of their wallet and not their heart.

When agent owned life companies are established, both the company and the producers are put in the position of wanting profitable business. Suddenly, the relationship is not on an adversary basis—it has become a partnership. This new type of compensation system can be so effective and so successful that it would not be unreasonable to see field marketing organizations becoming very large corporations. It would not be surprising to see some FMOs actually "going public" and selling shares in the operation.

Beyond compensation, there are other direct benefits that would work to the advantage of FMO members. For example, the power of the FMO could be used to help the agent obtain maximum support from the company issuing its business. Let's say you are an agent or PPGA writing business for a company that offers competitive products but has difficulty issuing policies promptly or correctly. How much power do you have as an individual producer? Will the company really care if it loses $40,000 in premium? What if you are part of an FMO that is giving the company $2 million in premium? Will the company listen if the organization complains? You bet they will, and they'll move quickly to shore up the problem.

FMOs—Not a One-Way Street

The key reason the FMO will be successful is that everyone involved—the agents, the consumer, and the companies—can all be winners. We've talked about the benefits for the agents—mainly that they can use their power of production to assure a positive relationship with the companies and receive compensation tied directly to their talent. Just as important, the agent's relationship is with people who know and understand his needs and wants. Because the FMO is made up of successful agents, there is little likelihood they would seek "alternative" distribution systems.

The companies are also big winners. By dealing with FMOs, companies can concentrate on doing what they do best, and that's manufacturing insurance coverage. The company/FMO relationship is very simple—manufacturer and distributor. Each participant in the arrangement performs the service it does best. Most companies are very good at developing products, processing applications, issuing policies, paying commissions, servicing the policyholder, paying claims, and developing computer reports to track all activity. In short, companies are good at generating paper. Companies are not very good at recruiting, motivating and training agents. Companies are inefficient at developing markets in which to sell their products. People in home offices are good at administration, not marketing, or they wouldn't be in the home office.

Companies working with FMOs can concentrate on what they do best and will not waste excess amounts of money in areas where they are inefficient. The company is able to view the distribution system objectively—as an operation that is separate and truly independent. This relationship will allow the companies to focus on the fact that their primary customer is the producer. The FMO relationship will enable companies to identify and concentrate their efforts on servicing those who can sell the products they produce.

The consumer will also be a winner in the new distribution arrangement because competition will mean better products, and an efficient distribution system will mean better service both at the point of sale and afterward.

Today's Promise—Tomorrow's Success

The idea of field marketing organizations is not a figment of this author's imagination. There are some very successful FMOs already in operation, and more are being formed every day. A good example of the FMO concept is an organization called Coordinated Planning Associates (COPA). This company, for that's the best way to describe it, is led by Mr. Robert Grebe, and produces nearly $10 million of paid premium annually. That's premium, not face amount! COPA concentrates on a simple life insurance saving sale, and with this concept has grown to 30 offices operating in 22 states. If COPA were a life insurance company, it would probably be listed as one of the fastest growing in the industry.

The COPA organization represents three different companies, recruits only non-experienced agents (about 400 per year), and provides no financing, except for annualization. The organization does offer some unique benefits to its associates. First, all prospecting and client servicing is provided for the agents by COPA. Agents are given a minimum of three scheduled appointments per night.

Second, because of the premium COPA produces, it is in a very strong position when negotiating with a company for services provided to associates. COPA concentrates in the lower income market and, as a result, thousands of people who could not be efficiently served by the classic career agency system are receiving personal service.

Of course, the field marketing organization is not limited to the lower income market. At the other end of the spectrum an organization called Cambridge Planning of Los Angeles works almost exclusively in the financial planning market. Mr. Fred Meyer started Cambridge Planning a few years ago and, by the end of 1985, the organization was producing life insurance premiums at the rate of $500,000 per week.

The key to Cambridge Planning's success, aside from the creative talent of a person like Fred Meyer, is the fact that it represents a number of companies offering a variety of products and services. In addition to making these products available to the financial planner, Cambridge Planning has very sophisticated systems for generating leads. Whether they are leads from a charitable giving seminar, or financial planning leads from a bank seminar, those working with Cambridge Planning can concentrate on what they do best, and that's selling.

A third field marketing organization called Agent Proposal Services of Peoria, Illinois, and managed by Mr. Derald Brocksmith, is effectively serving the middle income markets. The FMO was started in 1982 and today has contacts with over 6,000 agents. The organization provides thousands of quality leads by offering payroll deduction plans to nearly 100 groups. Working with Mr. Brocksmith agents find that one application per hour, rather than one per week, is the norm.

College Agency Management, led by Mr. Dave Sunderland; American International Marketing, under the direction of Mr. Grant Inkley; and Union Programs, organized by Mr. Don Purk, are all examples of this emerging new marketing structure. All these organizations produce multimillions of insurance premiums effectively and profitably, both for their associates and the companies they represent. Mr. John Holdaway runs a very successful (approximately $3 million in premium) nationwide FMO specializing in brokerage production.

While each of these successful organizations operates in its own unique fashion, they do share some common bloodlines. Each organization is led by very talented people, each is made up of individuals who are successful at selling insurance, and each has developed a special market in which to concentrate its efforts. In addition, most have developed systems that generate leads to increase the productivity of all member associates. But most important, they can offer competitive service and products to agents and consumers because they are independent of any company control.

David Kane, one of the more creative marketers in America today, and president of D.S. Kane and Associates, a field marketing organization producing in excess of $3 million in premiums, has written, "The formation of marketing organizations is one of the most dynamic changes occurring in the distribution of life insurance products in America today." Further on Kane noted, "People in the best position to evaluate how life insurance is going to be sold in the future are those people that sell it today successfully. Many of the brightest and most innovative minds in America are running marketing companies."[9]

The field marketing organizations will change the landscape of the distribution system, but they will not do it at the expense of the agent. FMOs will succeed because they have developed strategies that give the agents a chance to use their talents in a way that will allow them to survive and thrive. Agents who are concerned about the structure of insurance distribution in 1990 will do well to explore the benefits offered by forming or joining with other professionals in a field marketing organization.

Chapter VI Notes

[1] Charles W. Brodhead and Howard S. Cogan, "If You Can't Sell Your Image, You have Nothing to Sell!" *Life Association News,* June 1985, p. 75.

[2] "Issues and Outlook for the Ordinary Insurance Distribution System," Life Insurance Marketing and Research Association, Inc., 1983, p. 7.

[3] *Ibid.,* pp. 20-21.

[4] "North American Life Annouces Transition," *National Underwriter,* Life and Health edition, July 9, 1983, p. 15.

[5] James C.H. Anderson, MAAA, ASA, FCA, "Charting the Direction of the Life Insurance Industry," *Emphasis,* Tillinghast, Special Issue, July 1983, pp. 4, 5.

[6] Thomas M. Maher, "Financial Counseling: Insurers Ranked Last," *National Underwriter,* Life and Health edition, December 10, 1983, p. 2.

[7] "Merrill Lynch's Big Dilemma—Its Strong Broker System is a Costly Handicap in a Deregulated World," *BusinessWeek,* January 16, 1984, pp. 60-67.

[8] "Issues and Outlook for the Ordinary Insurance Distribution System," *op. cit.,* p. 12.

[9] David S. Kane, "Marketing Organizations: What They Are and What They Have to Offer," *Broker World,* September/October, 1984, pp. 86, 92.

7

THE AGENT'S ALTERNATIVE DISTRIBUTION SYSTEMS

In the previous chapter we studied the pressures being placed on the life insurance industry's traditional distribution systems, and explored the possible emergence of field marketing organizations as successors to the classic career agency. As good as the FMO solution may be, the wants, needs, and requirements of agents in life insurance are too pluralistic for any one system to be perfect for everyone.

In this chapter, we will explore some of the other options that will be available to agents. Included in our discussion will be sponsored agencies, surviving career agencies and PPGAs. In a subsequent chapter, we will explore the favorite of everyone today, the Financial Planner.

Sponsored Agencies

The sponsored agency organization (SAO) will look and operate much like a classic career agency. Walking into an SAO you will find some agents on the phone setting up their appointments for the week; in the conference room a group of new agents will be attending a training class; a couple of agency members will be over at the coffee machine discussing plans for the upcoming convention; and some agents will be polishing off a few proposals. Yes, everything would look familiar, but in reality, the operations would be very different from the classic career agency.

First of all, unlike the traditional career agency that is basically owned by a life insurance company, most SAOs will be owned by financial institutions like banks, thrifts or credit unions. This means that agents will owe allegiance to the financial institution and its customers instead of the insurance company. Rather than working with just one company, agents will be licensed with and encouraged to write for a number of carriers.

Another difference between the career agency and the sponsored agency is that agents associated with the latter will have to do very little, if any, prospecting. Any prospecting that is done will be under the auspices and sponsorship of the financial institution. This arrangement will provide a tremendous advantage for the participating agents and will greatly enhance their productivity. It's one thing to search out a prospect and open up the conversation by saying, "Mr. Jones? My name is MacDonald . . . Bob MacDonald of Night Life of Las Vegas . . . I have an idea that has been of value to . . ." It's quite another to be given a prospect to call and open up the conversation with, "Mr. Jones? My name is MacDonald . . . Bob MacDonald . . . I represent National State Bank and we are calling all of our valued customers about an idea that has been of value to . . ."

Commissions paid to agents associated with SAOs will, from a percentage standpoint, probably be less than currently paid in a career agency. However, because agents will sell larger volumes of premium, net income will be considerably higher. Many agents will react negatively to the idea of lower commission percentages but we must remember that grocery stores accept dollars, not percentages. Consider this: if I could direct you to prospects who would see you on a favorable basis, had an acknowledged need, and had the money to buy the plan you proposed, would you be willing to give me 25 percent of each case? If the answer is yes, you could find happiness in a sponsored agency.

As we previously discussed in our chapter on banks selling insurance, the SAO owned by a financial institution does have some drawbacks and will not be right for everyone. Those who work for a sponsored agency will probably be employees of the agency or financial institution, and despite the fact this means group insurance, free office space and pension coverage, many agents may not feel comfortable as employees. If one looks at it objectively, though, they will see that career agents of a traditional agency are, in reality, captive employees of the insurance company. The only difference is the financial institution will admit the relationship while the insurance company tries, for a variety of reasons, to hide the employer-employee relationship.

Other agents might be concerned that an SAO will limit their creativity and the work will be boring. Who wants to sell mortgage insurance all the time? I don't think lack of flexibility and the single need approach should be a valid concern for the good agent. Leads provided by the financial institution will be "door openers" and, from there, the good agent will be able to develop a variety of needs and eventual sales. A mortgage sale could lead to a discussion of business insurance needs, the pension plan or coverage on the spouse. Some agents will take the leads, make some easy sales and a good living. Others will follow-up their leads, and make some easy sales, but they won't stop there. They will use creativity to sell additional products and grow very prosperous.

The one concern I have about sponsored agencies today is the philosophical management environment of many financial institutions. As previously mentioned, the tradition in banks and many other financial institutions is that no one should make more money than the president. While this attitude is changing, it is doing so slowly. There are many banks and thrifts that would find it very difficult to have agents working in a subsidiary agency making more money than the president of the institution. Also, because bank marketing philosophy is very passive, many good agents may feel frustrated by a failure on the part of the institution to take full advantage of available insurance sales opportunities. With experience, this attitude of passive marketing will also change, but it will take time.

In the meantime, the solution might be for the agent to associate with a sponsored marketing organization that is independent and not owned by the sponsor. The non-affiliated sponsored agency presents the best of two worlds for the agent looking for an environment close to that of the classic career agency. Under this arrangement, the agency would enter into a joint venture agreement with a sponsor to provide marketing expertise in exchange for an override on all business produced. In the past, this arrangement has actually proved to produce the best results for both the institution and the agency. From the agent's standpoint, he still has the endorsement of the sponsor, plenty of leads to follow-up and the opportunity to make an income which is not limited by the philosophy of the institution.

Of course, for this arrangement to work effectively, the agency must be independent both from the institution and the insurance companies providing the products. The only reason this arrangement will not become dominant is that eventually many of the sponsoring institutions, for a variety of not always valid reasons, will want to own and control the agency.

In the future, the SAOs will perform many of the functions now undertaken by the career agency. They will recruit new agents, train them, finance them (with leads), and create long-term career opportunities. The SAOs will be able to accomplish these tasks when the career agency cannot because they will have a productive system in which the agent can operate. Agents working for SAOs will spend most of their time selling, not looking for someone to sell. Like the career agencies before them, the SAOs will be the pipeline for the other agent distribution systems. Many agents may "graduate" into field marketing organizations, PPGA arrangements or financial planning.

Surviving Career Agencies

I've previously made the point that the classic career agency is passing from the scene and will shortly cease to be the dominant distributor of life insurance. Yet that does not mean career agencies will disappear from the scene. Whole life insurance is no longer the dominant product of the industry, but it has not disappeared. One of the reasons career agencies will continue to exist is because they are generally associated with the largest companies in the industry that, if they want, can continue to subsidize the agency even while they invest money looking for alternative distribution outlets.

Most career agency companies have no valid way to measure the profitability of their agencies. They do know, however, the new interest sensitive products will reduce whatever profitability does exist. While these companies look for what they view as more profitable alternative systems, they will continue to pour money into the career agencies. The career agencies that do survive will continue the current trend of forcing the agents into higher and higher income markets. Agents associated with these agencies will generally sell the evolving investment oriented, interest sensitive products that will require NASD and SEC registration.

Consistent with this approach is the strategy of magically transforming the career agents into financial planners. Even now, New England Life's second leading volume agency identifies itself as "Baystate Financial Services." This strategy is fine as long as it is recognized and acknowledged. We must understand that such a strategy is not saving the life insurance career agency but changing it into something different. Again, there is nothing wrong with this unless the objective is to appear to be a financial planner so more life insurance can be sold. As we'll see later, attempting to save the career agencies by hiding behind the financial planning cloak can be very dangerous for both the company and the agent.

While higher income markets can result in larger sales, this approach is somewhat self-defeating. The agent working in the high income market will have to be very sophisticated, be required to qualify for a number of licenses, and meet continuing education standards. Therefore, much more training will be needed before the agent can be productive. This will call for the company to make an even larger investment in the agency. As a result, we will see fewer and fewer inexperienced people being recruited by these organizations. This situation may present us with a very interesting irony. Today many companies are crying about the investment they make in new agents, only to see them "stolen" away by evil companies offering a different opportunity. (Higher commissions? Better products? Prospecting help?) We may see a time when the career agencies "steal" the best agents of sponsored agencies by offering a different opportunity. ("Hey, you, come with us and you too can be a financial planner." What goes around sometimes comes around.)

Those agents who continue to operate in the classic career agency must accept the fact that the primary company, in order to recoup its major investment of time and money, will be pushing for higher and higher (and some may consider unreasonable) sales volumes. Just how successful this approach will be, both for the agent and the company, is still to be determined.

Personal Producing General Agents

In spirit and deed, the personal producing general agent is the essence of the life insurance industry as we like to think it is and as it should be. Think back to the time you were recruited into the life insurance business. Do you recall the key points of that first recruiting interview? Remember the recruiter telling you the best part of a career in life insurance is the opportunity to "be your own boss" and "to get paid what you are worth, not what the job is worth"?

Those were the reasons many of us became agents, but that's not what we got. As a career agent on a financing plan, we soon found out we weren't our own boss and were paid only the level of commissions the company felt they needed to pay. We were told when to be in the office, the time to be at sales meetings, the nights we should be calling and all the rest. We were far from being our own boss. And to be fair, as a new agent, receiving such supervision was probably the only reason I survived in the business. Left alone as my own boss, getting paid what I was worth would have been a sure prescription for failure and poverty.

The problem was that no matter how good we became at the job of being an agent, we could never be truly independent or have full freedom of earnings as part of the captive career agency system. We were basically limited to the products of our career company and were paid at the same commission rate as all other agents. Sure, we could earn more money than the next agent, but only if we sold more premium. If we took less of the general agent's time, should we then get a higher percentage commission? The GA paid all housing expenses, but maybe we didn't need an office on Wilshire Boulevard. If we made that decision, should we get the resultant savings? Good questions, but the answers were not there in a career agency system.

Yet the answers were there for the PPGA! Being a personal producing general agent has been the ultimate reward for the successful producer. The PPGA contract is the vehicle for the individual who seeks to realize the promises of freedom and independence offered by the life insurance industry. A very strong case can be built for the premise that a PPGA has the best job in the life insurance industry.

If that's the case, what exactly is a PPGA? Why isn't everyone a PPGA? If we were to play the word association game with PPGA, the first thought that would come to many of us would be—higher commissions. We tend to believe the higher commission contract is the magic of the PPGA. Actually, most successful PPGAs would probably tell us the commission levels are important yes, but there are many equal or more attractive factors.

Some PPGAs may make less net income than they did as career agents because those "higher" commissions must be used to pay expenses previously covered by their company agency.

Even if this is the case, however, the opportunity to be independent, the chance to control one's destiny, and the possibility of making more money from a well-run agency is just too much of an appeal for some to resist. To my way of thinking, the PPGA is the last of the true, rugged individualists in the life insurance industry. The PPGA typifies the entrepreneurial spirit of America at its best. The risk of failure is high, but the rewards, both physically and monetarily, are great.

The first adjective used by many PPGAs to describe their situation would be—independent. The true PPGA is out on his or her own, working alone or with a small staff. The PPGA earns his way, in the real sense of the word, by paying all expenses and sales support programs out of earnings. A majority of the business sold goes with one or two companies, not because the PPGA is obligated to them, but because the companies earn the business with competitive products and services. The real PPGAs are beholden only to themselves and their clients. They are truly their own bosses and get paid based on what they are worth to themselves and their clients.

Despite the benefits and freedoms offered by the PPGA concept, it's not right for everyone. Successful PPGAs may have the best job in the life insurance industry, but they also have the most difficult. Very few of us have the combined talents of a good salesperson and sound business manager, and those attributes are absolute requirements for success as a PPGA. Becoming a PPGA will enable successful agents to achieve more of the same but, in and of itself, it is not a solution to prospecting or selling problems. A PPGA is not the alternative for those who simply don't like their general agent.

In fact, in today's world of rapidly changing financial services and deregulation, it's becoming more and more difficult to survive as a PPGA. That's too bad because if there is anything the life insurance industry needs today it's successful, independent producers.

As we've seen at almost every turn, the agency system is under attack. The entire agency system is under attack, but it's the PPGA system that seems most threatened. With costs increasing and profit margins on new products being shaved, companies are seeking to maintain profit levels either by attempting to exert even more control over agents, or by searching for "alternative" distribution systems that will allow them to eliminate the agents. The independent PPGA is anathema to these approaches and many are going to try and squeeze him out of the business. Arrayed against the independent PPGA are the full resources of companies trying to develop all types of mass marketing efforts; companies pushing their captive agents into financial planning, the entrance of banks into insurance distribution, and the financial service centers like Sears. Not a pretty picture!

What is happening to the PPGA is very similar to what happened to neighborhood grocery stores with the advent of the supermarket. Thousands of local stores were squeezed out by the big supermarket chains. The independent stores did not have the resources to compete and were forced out of business. However, as we saw later, the local stores lost not because of the power held by the giant chains, but because they were not prepared for the changes taking place in the food industry. They were caught off guard and failed. If the PPGAs don't recognize the changes taking place in their industry and get caught off guard, many will meet the fate of the independent grocer.

Fortunately, there is a good side to the story. Today, in the name of 7-Eleven, Shop-Rite and a score more, there are more local and independently operated community grocery stores than anyone ever dreamed possible. Those stores that did survive and grow did so because they beat the big guys at their own game. The survivors carved out a niche in the marketplace that the chain stores couldn't meet. The independent operators banded together to make mass purchases of items so they could compete on price. They offered the convenience and personal service not available at the big supermarkets. Today we don't call these stores grocery stores, rather they are referred to as convenience centers. What a great marketing story! If these independent retailers tried to compete as grocery stores, they would lose. As convenience stores they serve a specific market and, as a result, not only survive but thrive.

I'm suggesting the same opportunity awaits the PPGA. The PPGA can meet the challenges of the financial services revolution, and come out a clear winner. To do this, the PPGA is going to need innovation and the use of state-of-the-art marketing techniques and technology. The beauty of all this is that, in survey after survey, the consumers tell us they respond best to personal service and want to buy their insurance from people, not machines. Like the local grocer, the PPGA is in the perfect position to provide objective, personal and convenient service.

The PPGAs can survive but I believe they will have to band together with other independents such as property and casualty agents, an investment advisor or tax shelter specialist. Each individual will specialize in an area of expertise and by working together as a team, they can provide the same services as the larger companies while maintaining their own independence. Such an arrangement may not pose a threat to the financial superpowers, but at least the PPGA will be able to compete. We will also see PPGAs joining forces to build their own field marketing organization. Under this plan, an organization would be formed to negotiate various contracts, service the producer's business and help develop prospecting systems. Each PPGA would maintain his independence while benefiting from the clout offered by the combined premium volume.

As we've already discussed in detail, in the not too distant future banks and other financial institutions will be allowed to distribute insurance and other financial products. While these institutions will be very successful distributors of insurance, there are also certain people who don't want to deal with the very large, and sometimes impersonal, services of financial institutions; the PPGA can fill this void.

I'm not suggesting that the idea of working with other independent professionals or field marketing organizations is the final or, for that matter, the only solution to the challenges facing PPGAs. The beauty of the PPGA system is that there is no one single answer. The PPGAs are free to use their unique abilities and creativity to find new opportunities where others only see threats. The key will be to keep ahead of the changes and not be swept aside. The PPGA of today, like the local grocer of yesterday, has something to offer the insurance buyer that's not available from any other source—convenient, objective, personal service. The PPGA who recognizes this advantage and plays to it, will not only survive, but like the convenience store, will prosper.

Distribution as the Hub of Life Insurance

The future distribution structure will be the life insurance industry's answer to the airline's "hub" system. When the airlines were heavily regulated, and costs could easily be passed along to the consumer, efficiency of passenger travel and transfer was not essential. As a result of deregulation, though, the airlines had to develop a more efficient system of distributing passengers along their systems. They became much more interested in keeping the traveler on the same airline for the entire trip. Airlines found the best way to do this was by simultaneously bringing all passengers into a central point and systematically transferring them out on another flight. TWA has developed St. Louis as its major hub, Republic uses Memphis and Delta centers its activity around Atlanta. The hub system has been successful in providing the airlines with a better chance of keeping the traveler for the entire trip. The field marketing organizations, sponsored agencies and, to some extent, the PPGAs of the future, will serve as a type of hub prospecting system for the agent.

Because the new organizations will specialize in a specific market to make prospecting easier and thus the agent more efficient, a whole variety of sales may spin off from the initial contact. For example, a bank may be the hub of sales because it can provide leads for mortgage sales, but like the airline that transfers the traveler from one company flight to another, the mortgage lead will generate a variety of other sales opportunities. The salary savings lead developed from the prospecting program of an FMO could lead to a mortgage or disability income sale.

All future distribution systems will have a hub prospecting concept that will serve as the core of sales but, for the good agent, that will not be the end of the sales opportunities. Just as the airlines have become more efficient and profitable by using their new hub concept, agents of the future will be more efficient and profitable using their new system of prospecting as a base.

8

SO YOU WANT TO BE A FINANCIAL PLANNER?

As personal income increases, economic and tax situations become more complex, and the variety of financial products expands, consumers are bombarded with a myriad of financial decisions. In such an atmosphere the need to seek help from someone schooled in all financial areas becomes a necessity.

As a result of the increasingly complex financial alternatives faced by many of us, there has been an explosion in the number of people who seek to be recognized as financial planners. There are estimates that the total number of people calling themselves financial planners is approaching 250,000. In the last five years, the membership of the International Association for Financial Planners (IAFP) has increased from less than 5,000 to 22,000. In the same period of time, the College for Financial Planning in Denver, Colorado, has granted over 9,000 Certified Financial Planner (CFP) designations, and has several thousand currently enrolled. The American Society of CLU has conferred the Chartered Financial Consultant (ChFC) designation to over 11,000 new financial planners. The number of individuals attending the annual convention of the IAFP now exceeds the number of those attending the annual NALU meeting.

All of this growth has not happened in a vacuum. There is a real need for professional financial planning, and the financial planner has the opportunity to join the lawyer and the CPA as a third professional in the personal services industry. Still, it won't come easy!

A financial planner is an individual who has the knowledge, experience, and the capability of developing an objective, balanced financial plan once all economic needs and goals have been identified and analyzed. The financial planner should be capable of long-term planning for investment, tax, retirement and life insurance needs.

I'm talking about the true financial planner. There are politicians who call themselves statesmen, garbage collectors who call themselves sanitation engineers, and life insurance salespeople who call themselves financial planners—but they are what they are. Anyone who calls himself a financial planner just so he can sell oil tax shelters is not a financial planner. Anyone who calls himself a financial planner just so he can sell more stocks is not a financial planner. Anyone who calls himself a financial planner just so he can sell more insurance is not a financial planner.

In order for the financial planner to become recognized as the true third professional, I believe there will have to be some form of formal certification, and services will have to be provided exclusively on a "fee-base" system. Only under a fee-basis arrangement will the client fully accept the concept of the planner being objective. When an individual making a recommendation will benefit financially from that action, it is very difficult to be totally objective. Even if the planner is totally objective, there will always be a question in the mind of the client.

In addition to operating on a fee only basis, the financial planners are going to need a way to better crystallize, possibly in their own minds and certainly in the mind of the consumer, exactly what it is they have to offer. When *Forbes*[1] runs an article on financial planners and pictures a monkey in a three-piece suit on the cover, you know the image of the financial planner needs some clarification.

The recommendation by the International Association for Financial Planners that a Self Regulatory Organization (SRO), similar to the NASD, be established to supervise financial planners will go a long way to improve the image of the financial planner. The idea of the SRO is to provide the consumer with the ability to identify who is, and who is not, a financial planner. Certain levels of disclosure and competence will be established. It was only after stockbrokers were able to establish such an SRO—the National Association of Securities Dealers in 1940—that they were able to regain the confidence of, and credibility with, investors that had been lost during the depression of the 1930s. Of course, a financial planning SRO, just like the NASD, will not be able to prevent unscrupulous individuals from entering or taking advantage of the financial planning shield. However, it will provide a unified supervisory system and provide some basis of measurement for the consumer.

It disturbs, but does not surprise, me that some of our old friends, the leaders of the National Association of Life Underwriters, have immediately come out against just such registration. Jack E. Bobo, NALU Executive Vice President, virtually acknowledged that some want agents to sell insurance by hiding behind the financial planning banner when he wrote, "To the extent that the public is more comfortable discussing insurance in the context of a financial plan rather than in the framework of death and disability, the result will likely be a better insured public. People have always resisted discussions that bring them face to face with the grim realities of life, therefore, it is always helpful to do so when such barriers can be minimized."[2]

Unbelievable! Is it any wonder that we in the life insurance industry have such a low public image and weak credibility with the consumer when national leaders suggest the best way to sell insurance is in a different "context"? I recognize the NALU is not the only organization expressing opposition to the establishment of a financial planning SRO. The other opposing arguments are based on either an intramural struggle among financial planning organizations, or on the belief that current regulations, which are extensive, are satisfactory for proper supervision.

As David Zeckets, CLU, ChFC, former insurance agent and currently president of a financial planning firm called Coordinated Planning Services has written, "The financial planning business is saturated with rejects from many other businesses. There are many people who enter the financial planning business who are not motivated to plan, but who are not happy with the business in which they are working. These people see the financial planning grass as being greener. Some of these people think, 'I can't sell life insurance, so I'll be a financial planner.' Mr. Zeckets makes the point that he is not picking on insurance agents, and goes on to write, "The new financial planner must be realistic. He can't be running away from his current career, but instead he must have an honest desire to build on that current career. Becoming a financial planner will not make the life insurance agent more motivated, an instant success, or even well-liked at cocktail parties."[3]

It is my belief that an SRO, even if not in the exact format as proposed by the IAFP, will be of more value to the life insurance agent in establishing financial planning credibility than it will be to the stockbroker, lawyer or CPA. The lawyer and the CPA already have the credibility of their professions and the stockbroker's credibility is enhanced by regulations under an existing SRO. It is the life insurance agents who, no matter how hard they try, will still be viewed as just trying to sell life insurance unless they can point to qualification under an SRO. The CLU, ChFC, and CFP are all nice and well-earned designations, but they will never carry the same weight for the life insurance agent turned financial planner as will "official" registration under an SEC supervised SRO.

Right now, life insurance companies and agents are not recognized by the consumer as a viable source of financial services or planning. In a 1983 survey consumers were asked "Imagine that you were looking for the service listed below. Please indicate the places where you would be likely to go (multiple responses.)" Under the category of "financial counseling" 45.2 percent said banks; 32 percent said CPAs; 13.2 percent listed lawyers; and 2.2 percent said they would turn to insurance companies. In the category of "investment counseling" banks again scored the highest response rate at 27.2 percent; CPAs were next at 20.9 percent; lawyers were listed by 8.4 percent; and insurance companies trailed with 2.4 percent. Even in the field of "estate planning" only 4.6 percent of the respondents indicated they would look to insurance companies; 13 percent listed CPAs; 15.9 percent would turn to banks; and more than 68 percent said they would follow the advice of a lawyer.[4]

My point is that certification under an SRO will not necessarily mean the individual will do a better job of financial planning than the person not so designated, but the perception of the consumer will be enhanced. And, perception is a large part of the acceptance battle for the life insurance agent turned financial planner. One other argument for an SRO is that such an organization will provide consistent qualifications for the financial planner. Due to the explosion in the number of people calling themselves financial planners, states are beginning to consider regulatory legislation. If this movement progresses, we could end up with 50 different definitions and a wide-variety of qualifications for the financial planner.

It would be nice to have the professional financial planner recognized on the same prestigious level as the lawyer and CPA, but failure to gain such recognition will not prevent success or service to the consumer. As long as a person operates on the basis of integrity and disclosure, there is nothing inconsistent with being a financial planner and selling products on a commission basis. The objective should be a successful financial plan, not "creating" a need or selling a preconceived product as the solution to all needs. There is nothing wrong with a person whose primary objective is to be a financial planner selling life insurance or any other financial product. Life insurance, stocks, tax shelters and other investments will all play key roles in a properly developed financial plan. Problems occur when a person whose primary objective is to sell life insurance, stocks or tax shelters, calls himself a financial planner.

The need and opportunity for financial planners will expand, but it should be noted that the market is fairly small. I doubt those who will need the services of a financial planner will ever exceed 5 percent of the population. It's difficult to see individuals making less than $75,000 needing many of the products or the expertise of the professional financial planner. The facts of life are that middle income consumers simply won't have the excess, spendable income necessary to buy enough of the financial planner's services or products to justify the planner's time. The exception may be working with the famous "Yuppie" generation where the combined income of the spouses is $60,000 to $70,000. Because this group will fall between individuals who can best be served by professional agents and the financial planner, it will be serviced by both. The fact that middle income individuals won't be good prospects for financial planners does not mean they don't need professional assistance. I believe most of these individuals will be better served by professional life insurance agents who will offer modern, flexible and competitive interest sensitive products.

Hatching the Financial Planner

While many bankers are moving into what they call financial planning, we must be careful not to confuse this with trust planning. My discussion of financial planning assumes full-time activity and, as a result in the future, many of the true financial planners will be lawyers or CPAs who have expanded or decided to specialize their practice. There will be plenty of opportunity for stockbrokers and insurance professionals who want to expand their market to those with high incomes. Those insurance professionals who are successful in moving from insurance sales to full financial planning and gain acceptance from the consumer will, in all probability, be the most successful.

No one is more capable than the well-trained life insurance agent when it comes to getting before a prospect, soliciting information in the fact finding process, and motivating an individual to take action on a proposed plan. In a country where 80 percent of the population does not even have a will, such training and talent will be very useful, if not essential, in successful financial planning.

Stockbrokers or insurance agents who become financial planners will operate in ways very similar to insurance distribution organizations. Some financial planners will develop independent practices much like personal producing general agents. In fact, most financial planners will be PPGAs to some insurance companies. Those who work as fee only planners will act much as the "team leader" in developing the financial plan. This person will coordinate the efforts of the lawyer, CPA and life insurance agent. If the individual personally sells any specific products the commissions will be fully disclosed and credited against the charged fee. (The anti-rebate laws are another reason fee only planning is difficult to offer today.)

Most independent financial planners will operate on a fully disclosed commission basis, offering long-term personal service to the high income individual. While some financial planners will work with, or out of, banks and other financial institutions, I do not believe banks will play a major role in offering financial planning. This is because most of the bank's regular customers fall in the $20,000 to $60,000 income group. Of course, those with higher incomes do business with banks but they are more likely to have personal advisors, such as independent financial planners, and will not look to banks for such service.

Quite possibly the largest group of financial planners could come from those life insurance agents operating out of the old career agencies. As we've seen, companies operating career insurance agencies are attempting to move agents into higher income markets and are beginning to offer a wider array of financial products. Equitable, John Hancock, and New England Life already advertise themselves as "financial services companies."

The American Society of CLU has created a Chartered Financial Consultant designation. In a series of national ads, The American Society of CLU now refers to itself as "the largest body of financial planners in the world." This strategy can work if the companies are really serious about converting their agencies from insurance operations into true financial planning organizations. Official certification of the financial planning service will give credibility to the companies and the agents who are attempting to make the transition from insurance only to financial planning.

The insurance industry has a well-deserved reputation for investment success, even if some feel such success did come at the expense of the consumer. The industry now has a chance to turn that image around by developing financial products and services that will fit well into the financial planning mode. To date, I hear much conversation, but I'm not sure real progress has been accomplished. Old habits die hard, and these companies still place a great deal of emphasis on life insurance. As Mr. Zeckets pointed out in his article, "Life insurance companies provide the greatest training in the world in the areas of sales and prospecting. But for some life insurance companies, their reluctance to join the investment world, their hypocrisy regarding term insurance and universal life, and their attitude that whole life is a panacea places them in a poor position. Life insurance companies make their money from insurance. No matter how many products they add, this fact never will change."[5] It may be difficult for companies to make the transition, but those who do will be able to carve out a profitable niche for the career agencies that survive.

As with other options emerging in the financial services revolution, a career in financial planning presents many opportunities but it should not be viewed as the best career option for everyone. As good as the opportunity in financial planning may be, it will not be the total answer to all of the life insurance industry's distribution problems.

Financial planning is just one of many ways the consumer will be served in the future. Simply being or calling yourself a financial planner will not mean the consumer will suddenly be beating down your door. (Police will still not have crowd-control problems outside your office.) It may cause a small boom in the market for three-piece suits, but there is no mystical success that goes with the financial planning title. And, as we've said before, hiding behind financial planning to sell a specific predetermined product will be the worst of all options. Financial planning will be the right option for some, but not for all. There is nothing wrong with being a financial planner but there is also nothing wrong with being a banker, CPA, or life insurance agent. The emerging and restructured financial services industry will create opportunity for all those who seek to offer the consumer honest, competent, objective service and competitive products.

Chapter VIII Notes

[1] "These Days Everyone's a Financial Planner," *Forbes,* October 8, 1984, front cover.

[2] Jack E. Bobo, CLU, "Ship Captain and Crew," *Life Association News,* August 1985, p. 10.

[3] David Zeckets, CLU, ChFC, "'So, You Want to be a Financial Planner . . .'" *Life Insurance Selling,* September 1985, pp. 42, 46.

[4] "Consumer Panel," *Better Homes and Gardens,* August 1983, Tables 195A, 195E, 195F.

[5] Zeckets, *op. cit.,* p. 48.

9

THE COMPANY—PARTNER OR PARASITE?

Only the individual agent can decide which distribution system best fits personal needs, interests and objectives. No single system can be best for everyone. However, there is one constant to all systems and that is the needed relationship with one or more life insurance companies. Just as companies will not be able to survive without the agent, agents also need the companies. The key for the agent is to pick the right company.

In the past, much like consumers buying insurance, agents stumbled into association with a company. Very few agents made a conscious decision to "shop around" for the best company to join. The prospective agent knew someone with a company—perhaps his own agent, responded to an ad, or was contacted directly by the general agent. As a result, the relationship between company and agent has generally been, at least contractually, a one-sided affair—with the odds stacked in favor of the company. Nevertheless, that does not mean the agent did not benefit from the relationship. Millions of individuals have had very rewarding and prosperous insurance careers because a company was willing to invest thousands of dollars in their development. The companies were willing to make that investment with little or no evidence as to the possible success of the new agent. Unfortunately, many companies seem to take the view that this investment allows them to treat the agent as an indentured servant for the rest of the agent's career. That relationship and attitude must change if both the company and agent are to be successful in the future.

Cats and Dogs

There are those who say the best way to improve the relationship between the agent and the company is to eliminate the adversarial relationship that seems to exist. I believe that's the wrong approach. We must recognize that agents and people who work in insurance company home offices are a different breed. Suggesting that all we have to do to improve the home office-field relationship is to stop fighting is a little like suggesting we make an effort to stop cats and dogs from fighting. The only way you're going to stop cats and dogs from fighting is by eliminating one or the other. That's not a good idea for either group. While both the field agents and the home office have the same long-term objective, the sale of the maximum amount of profitable premium, the short-term objectives of each are very different. Walter C. Duemer, president of a field marketing organization called Exceptional Producers, said before the 1985 CNA Executive Conference, "Agents and home office people have different needs, different objectives, different ways of solving problems." He added that, "Agents want exceptions, while home offices are tied to systems and procedures."[1]

This point was dramatically brought home to me in 1972, when I was appointed to the Field Advisory Council of Jefferson Standard Life. My job, as I saw it, was to represent the field force of the Western Region to the executives of the home office. Prior to my first meeting with the council, I contacted all the western managers and many of the top agents. I got their input as to what they felt were problems and specific steps needed to be taken by the company to help them be more successful.

The meetings were held at the Jefferson Standard home office in Greensboro, North Carolina. During the morning session, the home office executives told us about the great things happening at the company. Listening to them, it was obvious we were fortunate to be with such a fine company. In the afternoon, it was the field's turn. All the field representatives listed what were viewed as problems and offered suggestions for what we felt would be improvements in service. While we, especially I, were probably not as diplomatic as we should have been, I could not understand why the meeting broke up with most of the home office people yelling at us. What I failed to realize was that the home office viewed these meetings as primarily an opportunity to tell us of their problems with the field. To them, our job was to carry their message back to the field—not bring a message from the field to them.

Both sides sought the same objective—success for the company and the field—but the perspective from which we viewed achieving the end result was very different. In fairness to the Jefferson Standard home office executives, if someone from the field argued with me the way I argued with them, I would probably end up yelling, too.

Perspective in anything, but especially the relationship between an insurance company home office and the field agent, is everything. It's a little like the guy on the other team who is a dirty player until he's traded to your team. Then he's aggressive. Perspective! I've often thought the best way to improve the relationship between field and home office people would be to make each walk in the other's shoes for a little while. Possibly an underwriter would have more of a sense of urgency in issuing a policy if it was known just how hard it had been to get the applicant's signature. The agent might understand the problems of an underwriter if the agent had to review applications that were impossible to read, had incomplete information, or did not mention medical information that later came up in a Medical Inspection Bureau (MIB) inspection. Just maybe the home office financial people would not argue so vigorously against annualized commissions, (or for that matter, commissions) if they had to make their next house payment from a commission rather than a payroll check. The agent might understand the home office attitude a little better if he could count the number of "checks in the mail" that never seem to arrive.

I know that asking home office and field people to trade places is just wishful thinking, but it would be enlightening for both groups. We have to recognize that home office personnel and the field agent are always going to have a different perspective. And, in reality, there is nothing wrong with such a relationship. Most field agents would not be very happy or successful operating in the constrained atmosphere of a home office, and most home office people would not be very happy or successful trying to do the agent's job. Just as turning cats into dogs is not a good solution to that problem, turning home office people into agents or vice versa would not be a good solution. The home office and the agent must accept each other for what they are, and work out the best way to get along for mutual benefit.

It may be a little out of context here, but I'd like to take literary license and comment on one other aspect of field-home office relations. I realize that field people can become frustrated over what appears to be a noncaring attitude of many home office employees, but I'm continually amazed at how many successful salespeople forget who it is that actually runs a home office. Many field people are under the mistaken impression that the actions of the president or senior management of a company are the most important to their success with the company. I hate to admit it, but the management of a company—especially the president—probably has the least impact on the day-to-day success of an agent. From the agent's standpoint, the most important people in the home office are the clerical and supervisory people who do the real work and process the business. Agents who recognize this usually have the most comfortable relationship with a company.

Unfortunately, I've seen some very talented salespeople leave that talent in the briefcase when they talk to people in the home office. I'm surprised by the number of agents who call people in the home office and simply scream at them. The president usually gets very special treatment from the field, but if the agent must yell at someone, it would be better to yell at the president and give special treatment to the clerical people. After all, they are the ones who determine if and when a case gets issued or when the commissions get paid. I know a company should issue policies and commission checks as quickly as possible, regardless of personalities, but people in the home offices are, believe it or not, human. They respond very positively to human treatment. If agents will use some of their sales talent to "sell" themselves to the "key" people in the home office, they'd be surprised just how good the relationship could be.

Many agents have learned to send thank you letters and birthday cards to clients, but how many agents have ever picked up the phone or dropped a thank you note to a home office employee? I've known many agents who send flowers or candy to a doctor's nurse so an Attending Physician's Statement (APS) can get to the top of the pile, but what about the person who processes the business in the home office? Of course, I'm not suggesting bribery but I am suggesting some creative relationship building. If you are doing it you know what I'm talking about; if not, you might try it.

You Sing . . . I'll Dance

As I've stated before, the best way to reach the goal of a mutually profitable relationship is by having each group do what they do best. Simply put, the agent should spend time selling insurance and the home office should spend time manufacturing policies. There will never be a perfect relationship between the field and a company home office, but there can be a constructive partnership. If both sides recognize they need the other in order to achieve success, the relationship can be positive. The problem today is that many companies seem to think everything will be perfect if they can find a way to sell insurance without using the agent. And many agents act as though the companies are a bottomless bucket of money that can accept poor quality business forever. Neither belief is correct.

The best way for the field-home office relationship to work is to make sure it is a partnership. A successful partnership exists when each partner has a talent not possessed by the other, and each works hard to use his or her talent toward a common goal. It helps, but you don't have to like the other person to have a good partnership. Stan Laurel and Oliver Hardy never talked to each other off the set, but they had one of the most successful partnerships in show business because they needed and respected each other's talent.

In the future, agents must look for companies willing to enter into a true joint venture or partnership—not a pseudo employer-employee relationship. The company must be willing to assume the role of a manufacturer and let the agent be an independent distributor. This means the agent must identify companies whose corporate ego's do not get in the way. Lip service will not suffice in the new relationship.

A good example of this changing relationship will be seen in product development. Who knows better than the people selling them what products will sell? In the past, agents had very little say in the development of products. Product ideas usually came from the company, not the field. The company marketing department had a market it wanted to enter and went to the actuaries to create the product. After the product was developed, sometimes with little if any field input, it was given to the agents with instructions to "find a need." E. James Morton, President of John Hancock, underscored this point in a speech before the 1985 annual conference of the Life Office Management Association (LOMA) when he said, "But we still have a tendency, I'm afraid, to sit in our offices and invent new products and then go out and try to sell them. We are going to have to turn that around. We must begin doing what packaged goods companies have been doing for years—and that's to take a hard, careful look at what consumers want and need, and then develop those products, with the technology to support them, at a cost that will earn us a fair profit."[2] (John Hancock, of all the big companies, seems to be doing the best job responding to the challenges facing the life insurance industry.)

The manufacturer-distributor relationship will succeed in the future if the independent marketing organization with a market already developed, or in the process of opening one, can work with a company that will manufacture the needed product. The product ideas and specifications will come from the field, not the company. The home office financial people and actuaries have to develop the product and make sure it stays within lines of profitability, but they will function more as engineers than inventors. The actuaries and investment people will make sure all pieces of the product fit together, but they will not create the product concept itself.

Getting a company to use the right words is one thing, but finding a company to actually assume the limited manufacturing role is quite another. The relationship philosophy must be turned around, and that's hard to do. As Walter Duemer said, "It's an upside down organizational chart. Clients hire and fire agents. And agents will hire and fire companies—and have."[3] In contrast, this may be difficult for insurance companies to accept, especially after a century of having it the other way around. As Mr. Duemer continued, "Some insurance company executives may say, 'Wait a minute. Who's in charge here? I run this company. I'm the president. I don't need or want that agent telling me what to do.' "[4]

Agents must try to identify those companies who are willing to accept themselves as manufacturers and not distributors or financial service companies. Financial service is offered by the agent, not the company. The company should make the product, and the agent should offer the service.

We Have This Short Test We'd Like You to Take

For years, like the California surfer looking for the perfect wave, life insurance companies have used a myriad of tests trying to find the perfect agent. Most of us have taken the Aptitude Index Battery (AIB) test, the Merritt test, the "Canary" test, or scores of others. All these tests were trying to discover was whether we were worth the insurance company's investment of a few dollars.

Companies have yet to find the perfect agent, but they do have a certain set of guidelines that must be met before they will consider offering a contract. Agents should learn from the companies and establish their own tests looking for the perfect company. After all, agents are investing more than a few thousand dollars in the relationship—they are investing their talent and career. It may not be possible to develop a "test" that will find the perfect company, but agents can develop a certain set of guidelines that must be met before they will consider a company. Agents must make a conscious, intelligent decision as to which company or companies will best meet their needs.

In essence, agents must measure companies against three criteria: 1) product competitiveness; 2) efficiency of home office service and; 3) total compensation. It's one thing to make promises, but if a company cannot deliver those three basic services, the agent should look for another company.

By product competitiveness, I stress matching the product to the market being worked by the agent. American Airlines and Greyhound are both good companies providing the consumer with effective transportation services. However, both offer a different type of service. These two companies serve a different market and, thus, respond differently. In the future, agents will operate in much the same manner offering insurance products, but different products for different markets. The company must be willing to get away from the "off-the-shelf or nothing" product offering mentality of the past and be willing to develop special and individual products for the markets served by the agent.

As for home office service, as long as underwriting procedures stay the same, any company ought to be able to issue policies promptly and efficiently. But in today's world things do not stay the same. In the old days, we issued whole life or term and then term or whole life. Everyone used a standard application and followed the same nonmedical underwriting rules. In the future, however, all that will change and companies will have to respond.

First of all, even within one company, there will be a wide variety of insurance products being offered. Some products may use full underwriting, while others will require short form processing. Some policies will be direct billed and others will be list billed. In the past, many companies established their administration and computer support based upon the rigidity and sameness of service. As a result, they had a difficult time responding to a fluid market. Agents should examine a company based on its ability to do things differently and with flexibility.

From a commission standpoint, the key is for agents not to be charged for services they either don't need, or that duplicates what they are doing for themselves. As we mentioned in the discussion of field marketing organizations, the recruiting, selection, training and supervision of the agent will be transferred from the home office to the field. It is much more efficient to have these services provided by marketing organizations and they should be compensated in the commission schedules for such efforts. As Walter Duemer pointed out, "The biggest producers feel there is a redundancy in the services provided by home office and field. The escalating costs of company-provided services are recognized as a drag on commissions or as an expense which increases policy premiums."[5]

Companies usually build into the product a charge of anywhere between 10 to 20 percent of the premium as a "load" for the marketing department. (The home office financial types refer to these as "allowables"—the amount a department is allowed to spend on the business.) In essence, this is the commission paid by the company to the marketing department for the development of new premium. Agents should look for companies who are willing to pass along to the producer all or a portion of these allowances if the marketing department services are not used.

When examining companies, agents should look at the way they are operating today. Is the company comfortable working with field organizations that are not exclusive, and who may, in fact, be doing business with a number of manufacturers? Is the company effectively providing product, commission and support flexibility to its current field? Has the company ever developed a specific product for a specific marketing organization? Is the company willing to enter into "agent owned" company relationships? Does the company have a system for passing along the savings if the marketing organization does not require typical marketing support programs? Are the commissions "grossed" to the field organization so they, rather than the company, can determine how they will be distributed among the producers? Is the company willing to enter into joint venture financing arrangements without seeking ownership or control of the field unit?

These are all important questions that must be asked and answered before an agent agrees to a relationship with a company. Also, agents must look to those companies who are attempting to use modern technology and techniques to help the agent do the most onerous part of the sales job—prospecting.

Helping the Agent Prospect

I think we can all agree that the agent's natural strength is selling ability. Where the agent is less effective, however, is in follow-through, in administration and, not the least, in generating good leads in a cost-efficient manner. Some companies have made strides in relieving agents of certain servicing and administration tasks, and that's all to the good. In other cases, agencies themselves have invested in automating those tasks, and that is also to the good. But in the third and perhaps most critical area, generation of strong leads, progress has been slow, at least where agents are concerned. As we've pointed out, this is why we hear so many prophecies of impending doom for the agent. Forcing the agent to make all those cold calls is very expensive and frustrating for both the agent and the company. Agents should look for companies that are making a serious effort to solve this particular problem.

Earlier in this work, I was critical of some actions taken by Metropolitan Life but I must praise their acquisition of the Century 21 real estate operation. Now, it may be that Met will simply license the real estate agents to sell insurance, but the Century 21 deal has the potential for developing thousands of leads for agents. This action is certainly welcome and must be commended. We need to see more of this activity which will create leads for agents, not compete against them.

There have been some very dramatic developments in telemarketing and in the ability to develop leads on a mass marketing basis. I have attempted to avoid taking a parochial approach in this book, and so, have resisted talking about ITT Life and our specific programs. I must admit to pride, however, in the development of a telemarketing unit at ITT Life. This unit has two objectives: 1) generate leads for agents and; 2) attempt to reinstate business that has lapsed.

In essence, we set up a systems link between a computer, a group of telephones, a prerecorded message, and a live service person to follow up. The system sorts good leads from poor ones so the agent does not have to spend his or her far more expensive time doing the same thing. Using this technique we preselect the prospects that will be turned over to the agent and, in the process, we greatly improve the odds of converting prospects to sales. In addition, we make the system available to field units that have developed specific markets and lead sources. For example, one of our marketing organizations works under a sponsored arrangement with credit unions. The telemarketing unit is used to call the credit union members and set up appointments for the servicing agents.

ITT Life did not invent telemarketing, and we can't claim to be the first insurance company to employ the technique. In contrast, earlier applications that we looked at seemed far from perfect. In some cases, the computerization was so total and so intimidating that people thought they were dealing with robots and refused all further contact. In other cases, local agencies experimented with a more personal approach, but the marketplaces appeared too narrow for the law of large numbers to work in favor of generating new business cost efficiently.

Working with our field force, we developed an approach geared to our agents' specific markets and the products they sell. The system currently being used makes close to 500 calls per hour on 16 outbound watts lines. The computer monitors all calls as they are dialed, distinguishing among busy signals, rings and no answers. While computers are used for speed and efficiency, the prospect talks to specially trained operators, both at the beginning and end of each telephone contact. Many of the generated leads and sales appointments are sent via electronic mail to computers in our agency offices. This makes the leads available to the agency within hours of having been developed. Naturally, not every telephone call or lead translates into new business. But we have discovered that the trade-offs between overhead costs and new business development are excellent.

Even though ITT Life started the telemarketing program in 1982, we think the potential is yet to be fully tapped. There is still much work to do but we can see a time in the future when, working in conjunction with our field organizations, all prospecting and much of the service work can be accomplished using sophisticated telemarketing programs. The potential is endless. For now, we think we are taking action which will allow us to preside over the death of the cold call—not that of the agent.

Putting Out a Contract

If the relationship between the agent and the company is going to evolve into more of a partnership and joint venture arrangement, most agency contracts must be changed. The typical agency contract of today is so one-sided and onerous, it's a wonder they have been able to stand up in court. Agency contracts are an insurance company lawyer's dream come true. Reading agency contracts one could get the impression that company lawyers are taking all their frustrations out on the agent. This must change to a more equitable situation in the future. As Jim Tappe, CLU, an agent from Iowa, has written, "It is time agents banded together and refuse to deal with companies that have particularly onerous provisions in their contract. It would be good to develop a model contract that agents offer companies."[6]

I believe that improving agency contracts is just as essential to the preservation of the agent as improvements in productivity. Most agent contracts start with a clause that says something like, "You will exercise independent judgment as to the conduct of your business. The company's sales aids in no way constitute direction or control by (your company) over the manner and means of the conduct of your business." After trying to establish the "independent contractor" nature of the agent, mostly for the benefit of the company, the balance of the contract usually places strict control over the agent.

It is not my objective to dwell on this, but an example of a typical control clause found in some agency contracts would read, "(your company) may terminate this contract if, in its sole opinion, brokerage business is being conducted by you which is detrimental to the business purposes of (your company)." All judgment is left to the company and the agent has no recourse or protection. Much to their credit, the Ten Million Dollar Forum, the Million Dollar Round Table and Dr. Joseph Belth have all focused on this subject. In fact, the MDRT has published an "Agent's Contract Checklist" and it should be required reading for all agents.

Organizations seeking to do business with companies, especially the field marketing organizations and the independent sponsored agencies, should make contract negotiations just as important to their relationship with companies as they do product, commissions, and service. When organizations are in the position of controlling large amounts of premium, they should not give it away in a one-sided contract. Let me assure you that if the production unit is large enough, the company will be more than willing to negotiate the contract. The first thing an organization should do is read the contract or, better yet, have a lawyer read it. (If you are going to write much business, it will be worth the expense.) Large production organizations should consider the company's contract as the starting point in negotiations, not the end.

There is one other factor to consider and that is people working in companies sometimes leave and companies do change their marketing philosophy. You may have a particularly good understanding and relationship with the marketing officer or even the president of a company, but what happens if that person is not there? Contract provisions that did not seem especially onerous when you were dealing with one individual may become very difficult if that individual is not there. In today's world of heavy acquisition and merger activity, there is no guarantee the company will be around tomorrow. If a company will not give you a contract saying it will never change its marketing philosophy or distribution system (which it can't), then you should demand a contract that explains your rights and provides protection in the event it does change.

What happens if you are working with a company whose president is committed to the field marketing organization distribution system, but is replaced by a financial person who thinks direct mail is a better way to sell insurance? Under most contracts, you would have little recourse and be out looking for a new company. While that was taking place, the members of the FMO would be without a product and possibly without income. Now, don't think that such a situation has never happened; it has, more than once. This is another reason why I believe agents should avoid representing one company exclusively. The field organization working with more than one company will not be left out to dry if one of the companies changes direction. Leaders of field marketing organizations should also make sure the contracts recognize the fact that the organization and its members are truly independent of the company. Agents working with an FMO belong to the FMO, not the company. The contract signed by the FMO should clearly make that point.

Companies of the Future

The life insurance industry has been dominated by giants. Even though there are over 1,900 legal reserve life insurance companies in America, the five largest write over 20 percent of the business, and the top 100 companies write over 75 percent of the industry total. The listing of the top 25 companies changes very little from year to year. Just as there has been discussion of the agent as an endangered species, there are those who predict the demise of many life insurance companies. An article in the *Institutional Investor* said, "As for the life insurance industry itself, it will survive . . . but ten years from now it is likely to look very different from the way it does today. The old gentlemanly fraternity, fast crumbling in the current crisis, will be a thing of the past. Market shares will have been rearranged. There will be a radically altered distribution system, and many of today's companies won't be doing business anymore."[7] Arthur Andersen & Co. conducted a survey among life insurance executives for LOMA and found there will be significantly fewer smaller life companies. "All panels predict a 41% decline in the number of smaller life companies (by 1990), with a corresponding 28 percent decrease in market share."[8] There are some people who have predicted that due to mergers, acquisitions and plain failures, there will be fewer than 500 life insurance companies doing business by the turn of the century.

While I generally agree that there will be fewer full-service life insurance companies doing business in the year 2000, I also believe there is an opportunity for the smaller companies to grow. As Jim Anderson has written, ". . . there will also remain a larger number of specialty organizations, serving specific needs of various market sectors . . . Clearly, opportunities for the visionary exist, but clear vision, strong nerves and an enterprising spirit will be required to capitalize on those opportunities."[9]

I believe the successful smaller to medium sized companies will actually experience the best growth record in the industry. By the end of this century a number of today's smaller companies may begin emerging as the new giants of the industry. This conclusion is drawn because of the tremendous volatility present in the life insurance industry. In a period of stability it is very difficult for smaller companies, in any industry, to make much headway. Still, while change is viewed as a threat, it is more often a threat to the status quo than to those looking for new opportunities. Large companies set in their ways with tradition and bureaucracy usually have a more difficult time responding to shifting tides.

The younger, smaller, more aggressive companies are in a position to react quickly in a changing market, and those that make the right decisions will be very successful. Agents associated with these companies will be able to share in the benefits. The key will be to identify the companies that have the inclination to take advantage of the new opportunities, and also have the financial resources to implement their plans. Agents, for their own survival and prosperity, should examine companies closely—being careful to identify those who are responding to the opportunities available and, likewise, those who remain committed only to a time that has passed.

Chapter IX Notes

1 Sheril Arndt, "Agent's Aren't the Enemy, Exec Tells Insurers," *National Underwriter,* Life and Health edition, September 21, 1985, p. 14.

2 "LOMA Conference Report, 'Come Out of the Past,' Outgoing Chairman Morton Urges Colleagues," *National Underwriter,* Life and Health edition, September 28, 1985, p. 24.

3 Arndt, *op. cit.,* p. 14.

4 *Ibid.,* p. 14.

5 *Ibid.,* p. 14.

6 *The American Mustang,* The American Council of Independent Life Underwriters, April 1985, p 3.

7 Lynn Brenner, "Can the Life Insurance Industry Survive?" *Institutional Investor,* September 1981, p. 186.

8 "Changing Horizons for Insurance: Charting a Course for Success," Arthur Andersen & Co., and LOMA, 1984, p. 4.

9 James C.H. Anderson, "The Changing Financial Services Scene, *Tillinghast,* December 1984, p. 7.

10

THOUGHTS OF A TRAITOR

Framed on my office wall are the 16 different business cards I have used in my insurance career. The cards trace my activity as an agent with New England Life to president of ITT Life. I know many who think the display is simply an ego trip, and it may be, but to me these cards represent the opportunity available in the life insurance industry.

Life insurance is the only business I've ever known. At the age of 22, the life insurance industry offered me opportunity and promises available from few other careers. Like many others, I was recruited into life insurance with the promise that if "I would plan my work and work my plan" the opportunity to progress would be based, not on who I knew or what degree I had but on my ability alone.

At 22 years of age I was very young and impressionable. Within six months of becoming an agent, I knew life insurance would be my career and, believing the promises made to me, sat down to work out my plan. I established two long-term goals:

1) to be a general agent by age 30 and; 2) to be elected president of a life insurance company by my 40th birthday. It was then that I started saving my business cards. I knew that some day they would be framed on my office wall. The life insurance industry did not disappoint me. I became a regional agency manager for Jefferson Standard at age 27, and president of ITT Life at age 37. In the intervening 15 years, I worked as an agent, a unit supervisor, general agent, marketing services officer, senior marketing officer, chief operating officer and, finally, chief executive officer. Just as important during that period of time, the life insurance industry provided me the opportunity to get married and raise six children.

Of course, whatever success I have achieved did not come easy—I worked hard. Very hard. I can remember watching only one Monday night football game until I started working in the State Mutual home office. (That may tell you something about hard work in the home office.) But more seriously, there were the 15-hour days, the rejections, the small commission checks, the disappointment in seeing someone I brought into the business fail and, most importantly, the time away from my family. In those early years my wife and I suffered through some very heated discussions about the benefits of a career in life insurance. Fortunately for me there were also victories. I can still remember my first sale. (Some have suggested I had so few sales, I should be able to remember all of them.)

The life insurance industry gave me even more than was promised. My career has also provided me with the opportunity to meet and learn from a rainbow of personalities who could only exist in an industry like ours. I have been fortunate to have learned something from virtually everyone I met—even though from a couple of them it was learning what I did not want to do. (I'd like to list all the people who have helped me, but many of them are still active in the insurance industry and don't want it known that they know me.)

Of all the things I've done and of all the people I've met, my experiences as an agent and the opportunity to work with agents have been the most rewarding. Nothing in this business replaces the thrill of a sale. Unfortunately, the further along one moves in the life insurance industry, the further one gets from what the industry is all about.

Decisions I make today may not have any impact in the real world of insurance—where the agents work—for nine months to a year, if ever. Agents don't work in such a vacuum—they work in the real world. The biggest thrill I get out of the business today is when I receive a letter from one of ITT Life's agents telling me that what we are doing has helped him. All the frustration felt from working in the strange world of a company home office is washed away when an agent writes to me and says, "As far as I'm concerned, ITT Life Insurance Corporation is the finest insurance company in America today. The things your company continually does for us in the field amazes me. Our association with your company has changed my life and the lives of my close associates and our families like we never dreamed possible. You have given us all the opportunity to achieve standards of success we never thought could be attained in the insurance industry before." (Of course, I throw away the letters complaining about how we screwed up a case.) My wife, Patty, often reminds me that the best time we had in the insurance business was working with the agents in my agency. She says, "All those people were our friends. They were like our family."

I rarely go to industry meetings attended by other home office executives (you can't believe how boring they are) but I jump at the chance to meet and talk with agent organizations, especially the local groups, and our field agents. Addressing a group of agents—even if they don't agree with me—is very stimulating and it gives me the chance to get a feel for what's really happening in the industry. At industry meetings one can only get a feel for the industry as the home office executives would like to think it is, or as they think it should be. Rarely is reality an issue.

Yet despite my background, experiences and feelings, there are many who consider me a traitor to the life insurance industry. As I mentioned earlier, *Life Association News* has published three articles that specifically attacked me and my company. I've received scores of letters using such terms as "cesspool of the life insurance industry," "Antichrist," etc. Can you think of any person with 20 years of experience in the life insurance business (and who also happens to be president of a life insurance company) who has been declined membership in the NALU? I can. (My application for membership in the Minneapolis Association of Life Underwriters was also "declined." No reason was given.) I told you about one guy who wrote to the American Society of CLU and demanded my designation be revoked.

If I had a dollar for each time I've been called a traitor. . .! But a traitor to what? A traitor to an industry that had grown non-responsive to both the consumer and the agents? A traitor to a once good product that had outlived its usefulness? A traitor to companies who had grown lazy because of lack of real competition? A traitor to an industry that tried to teach agents to sell only on fear, guilt and emotion when the consumer had grown beyond that and wanted professional advice coupled with competitive products? A traitor to companies that said one thing to the agents while it searched out systems designed to eliminate the agents? A traitor because I suggested that agents must think and act for themselves?

For many, the answer to all those questions is a resounding "yes." Yet, if I was so far off the mark, why was there such a violent reaction? Someone once said you can judge the validity of new ideas by measuring the criticism leveled against them. New ideas that have no merit will be ignored and quickly pass from the scene, but new ideas or opinions that strike a chord will be vigorously resisted by those attempting to preserve the status quo.

A few months ago, after a speech before a group of agents, one of those in attendance stood up and asked, "What prompted you to take the risk of breaking away from the mainstream of the life insurance industry?" A great question. It may simply have been naiveté, but I never viewed the actions I and ITT Life took as being a risk. Looking back, I can see that many in my company, and certainly my superiors, felt we were taking a serious risk. However, I felt our actions were logical, honest and, if anything, late. If I and ITT Life had taken such actions in 1975—that might have been risky. By 1982, though, the things we said about the industry and its products were, or at least should have been, obvious to everyone. As far back as 1978, serious articles appeared in industry publications questioning the long-term future of whole life insurance. The concept of Universal life was already five-years-old. Canada had been selling a similar product for ten years and investment linked policies were the rage of the British market.

For anyone who wanted to look, there were some very obvious road signs indicating the life insurance industry had serious problems. Since the early 1970s, the percentage of whole life sold had been steadily declining. Industry lapse rates were climbing, the number of new agents entering the life insurance industry was declining, but more importantly, real agent income was being reduced.

Even more of a problem for the industry than the obvious signs of trouble with the traditional products was the consumer's growing negative perception of the industry. Members of the media were constantly writing and talking about the deficiencies of our products. Right or wrong, the Federal Trade Commission's report on life insurance had a negative impact. Surveys were constantly showing the industry losing credibility with the consumer. We can argue all we want about how good our service to the consumer may be, but if the consumer perceives it to be poor or non-responsive, then we have a problem.

I have a philosophy which says that sometimes the best time to take a risk is when you have the most to lose. From my viewpoint, the industry, the agent, and not least of all my company, had a great deal to lose if we continued to follow the path we were traveling. Just think about it—what was the life insurance industry doing in 1982 that it was not doing in 1930? In over 50 years, very little in the life insurance industy had changed. Yet, we all know the consumer and the economy changed a great deal during those 50 years. I have a plaque on my office wall which says, "If you are being run out of town. . . Get in front of the crowd. . . And make it look like a parade." To me, the real risk was to do nothing. By ignoring the crowd you could get trampled. It was Arnold Glasow who said, "Many a false step is taken by standing still."

There are some who may say, "All that's fine. But why did you have to go public and be so loud about it? Couldn't you have done your thing without attacking the industry?" Good questions. Frankly, we saw the industry's resistance to change and its dogged determination to hold on to whole life as a unique opportunity for ITT Life and our agents to compete effectively against the giants of the industry. We commissioned a very sophisticated market survey and discovered that we did not sell much insurance to other insurance companies. As a result of this revelation, we made a specific strategic decision to compete against, rather than with, the other companies.

From the reaction we got, we may have been the first company to make such a decision. As *The Hartford Courant* has written, "For decades, the life insurance industry was virtually devoid of real competition. Since there was plenty of business for everyone, each company settled into its market niche and took care not to tread on the turf of brother insurers."[1] William C. Scheel, Associate Professor of Insurance at the University of Connecticut, put it even more bluntly when he said, "I know of no other industry where companies are as closely associated as. . . insurance companies."[2]

Let's face it, the life insurance industry has been dominated by the large mutual companies. How could a 15-year-old, small stock company hope to make a mark in the industry by playing "me too" with the big companies? Fortunately, the big companies by their resistance to needed changes, opened a window of opportunity we were more than happy to enter. Of course, our strategy would have failed if the industry leaders had been more responsive to consumer challenges. Yet, because what we were saying was true, attacks against us by an industry that had lost credibility simply fueled our credibility. Privately, presidents of a number of small companies came to me and said, "You're right on. I wish we had done what you did."

One of the more amusing chapters in our "battle" with the industry was over the replacement question. I think we were the first company to publicly say it was okay to replace in force whole life policies. The reaction we received to our position on replacement was nothing short of a firestorm. Little did it matter that scores of companies, including agents from some of the most prestigious, had been replacing business for many years. It was just that the other companies had always been very quiet about their replacement activity. We were attacked only because we publicly condoned such activity. With all the fuss, one might think the only business ITT Life ever sold was replacement—but that activity never accounted for more than 20 percent of our total sales.

Battling the industry traditionalists on the product front naturally led to divergent viewpoints on other issues. When unisex pricing of policies became an emotional issue for the industry—we took an opposing stand. We did this, not just for the sake of arguing, but because we felt the industry was missing the point of the unisex question. We supported the industry on the retroactive aspect of the issue, but believed unisex was a social, not actuarial, issue. Also, unisex was nothing new to ITT Life; we had been selling unisex policies since 1975 and the walls had not fallen down.

When the big companies began opposing bank entrance into insurance distribution we figured they must know something—so we started working with banks. It's too self-serving even for me to talk about the success we have had, but let me just say that if we had to do it all over again, we'd do it in spades. As George Bernard Shaw said, "You won't learn to hold your own in the world by standing on guard, but by attacking and getting well-hammered yourself."

Most of those issues are behind us. Universal life has become a staple in the industry, many companies offer unisex rates while others admit they soon will, and scores of companies are trying to sell insurance through banks. As I've tried to say in this book, today we face issues that transcend all the problems of the past few years. At stake today is the very thing that made our industry great—opportunity for the agent. The promises made to me and millions of other agents are seriously threatened.

Successful, rewarding careers are threatened not because the agent has become outmoded, but because many company executives refuse to admit that the system under which the agent operates has become obsolete. Just as there were some who mistakenly felt the best way to save whole life was to raise policy loan interest rates, there are some who believe the best way to solve the industry's distribution problems is to eliminate the agent. I can't accept that logic. I believe agents and the industry deserve better.

If you've read this far, you know what I think has to be done to make sure the promises of a life insurance career do not disappear. You may not agree with all my suggestions, you may not agree with any of them, but I'm hopeful a discussion of the issues will help us find workable distribution answers for agents and companies.

There is one other point I'd like to address, and that's the status and prestige of the agent. Since we make people face issues they'd rather not and, because we sell, we will never receive the status and prestige of some other professionals. For those who work hard, are honest, and do their best to develop the proper insurance security program for a prospect, the failure of the public to give status to an agent's work can, to say the least, be frustrating.

In the last decade I've seen agents try to succeed by hiding who they are and what they do. A quick look at titles on business cards used by agents will make this point very clear. I must admit that as our products fell further and further behind the times and became less attractive to the consumer, disguises used by the agent were a natural course of action. But that approach didn't work. Calling ourselves something we are not will not fool the consumer for very long. Demonstrating embarrassment about what we do or sell only makes us weaker in the eyes of our customers.

No matter how romantic or fancy the various financial products become, the fact remains that people still need and want protection. Those who provide that protection perform an important and valuable service. The life insurance industry is now developing products we can once again be proud to sell. Sure, there will be those who will become Financial Planners. They will perform a valuable service for the consumer, but they will serve only a portion of the total financial services market. The vast majority of Americans will need the services and products that only a well-trained, independent, professional agent can offer.

We should be proud to be in the life insurance business. When we accept ourselves for what we are and what we can do, we will then have a much better chance of being accepted by the people we seek to serve. We face unsettling times, but these are times of opportunity and reward for the person who knows what he wants to do and has the courage to act.

As a final point, I firmly believe that agents cannot take the future for granted. It may not be easy, but agents must not sit by and let others make the decisions that will determine the future structure of the insurance industry and the role of the agent. Agents have tremendous power. Agents are the only people who can successfully sell large volumes of life insurance. Without agents, the life insurance industry will atrophy and die. Agents should work together to take advantage of their power, not abuse it, and to assure that they and the agents who follow will have the opportunity to achieve the success warranted by their efforts and talent. In short—agents should plan their future and work their plan.

Chapter X Notes

[1] "New Insurance Offering Signals End of Harmony in Industry," *The Hartford Courant*, Hartford, CT, June 7, 1981, pp. A1, A23.

[2] Ibid

ACKNOWLEDGEMENTS

This book offers a personal commentary on the life insurance industry. It was written by Bob MacDonald the individual—not Bob MacDonald the president of ITT Life. The thoughts and ideas expressed in this book are mine (at least the ones that I have not stolen) and do not necessarily represent those of ITT Life, The Hartford Insurance Group, or ITT Corporation. Since this has been a personal endeavor, these organizations have not been provided with the opportunity to formally review or comment on the manuscript prior to publication.

It is not my intention to make money off agents; all income derived from the sale of this book will be donated to charity.

Despite the disclaimer above (which is true) this book would not have come to fruition without a tremendous amount of help from a list of people almost too numerous to mention. (In order to protect the innocent, I will not list them.) To all I offer my sincere thanks. Thanks also to my wife, Patty, and the children: Ryan, Brandy, Piper, Colin, Braden, and Bo for all the lost evenings and weekends while I struggled to put my ideas in some understandable format. A special bit of thanks is extended to my longtime secretary, Jo-Anne Halek, for spending her personal time to correct thousands of spelling, grammatical and punctuation errors. As you have discovered, I am not a natural writer. If this book was at all readable, Jo's editing ability deserves the credit.

I also want to take this opportunity to offer special thanks to the field marketing directors, general agents, agents and all employees of ITT Life. During the last nine years, it has been my privilege and pleasure to have been associated with this outstanding group of people.

During that period of time, by working together, we have been able to move ITT Life from a little known credit and health insurance company to one of the best known, most aggressive, innovative and successful companies in the life insurance industry. To me, these accomplishments demonstrate just how powerful a true field-home office partnership can be. The creativity, independence and challenge of the field force combined with the hard work, loyalty and dedication of the home office staff created for me an unbelievable atmosphere of stimulation. It's been fun, and to all of my field and home office associates, I offer a special thanks.